The Herbal
Home Companion

The Herbal
Home Companion

Theresa Loe

KENSINGTON BOOKS

KENSINGTON BOOKS are published by

Kensington Publishing Corp.
850 Third Avenue
New York, NY 10022

Copyright © 1996 by Theresa Loe

Kensington and the K logo Reg. U.S. Pat. & TM Off.

First Kensington Printing: September, 1996
10 9 8 7 6 5 4 3 2 1

ISBN 1-57566-085-7

Printed in the United States of America

To my parents,
who have always given me strength and encouragement.
And to my husband, Rick,
who offers his love and support in everything I do.

A very special 'thank you' goes out to:

My husband, Rick, who kept me "fed and watered" through the long, grueling hours at the computer and who was always willing to try my next culinary creation (especially the lemon ones). My mother, Betty Neff, not only for her support and enthusiasm, but for opening my eyes to the joys of cooking and crafting at a young age. My father, George Neff, for always having faith in my abilities and encouraging me to see my inner strength. My grandmother, Nada Grosshans, for being my gardening confidant. My sister, Carrie Christine, not only for being one of my recipe testers, but for diligently keeping the recipes "top secret." My brothers, Jimmie and Gary Neff, for their loving support and their willingness to taste recipes with "green things in them." My dear friend, Renee Mustard, who not only tested more than her share of recipes, but who acted as my personal cheering section from the very beginning. Another dear friend, Lisa Shaddox, who diligently used her gardening knowledge to proof numerous chapters and help research many of the botanical names. Betsy Amster, for her insightful guidance and faith in my abilities. Beth Lieberman, for her professionalism and assistance. Monica Harris, for her meticulous work and herbal enthusiasm. Linda Chlup, for her artistic expertise. Wendel Withrow, for his ardent proof reading and editing. Dr. Art Tucker, for his unequaled botanical nomenclature expertise. And last but not least, to my other wonderful recipe testers who made and subsequently ate everything edible in this book: Demitra Christine, Leslie Loe, Pattie Mucciolo, Brian Mustard and Lauren Mustard.

Contents

⌘

Introduction

More than any other type of plant, herbs awaken our senses. Their foliage and flowers offer unequaled fragrance, texture, flavor, and beauty. What's more, they have unlimited usefulness for the home, body, and spirit.

From the ancient Egyptians with their ointments and perfumes, to the Victorians with their herbal fragrances and floral displays, people have utilized these plants for centuries. Herbs are rich in history and tradition. The folklore and superstition associated with each herb is fascinating. Even some of their old-fashioned names reveal this folklore and conjure up all kinds of romantic images. Can't you just imagine a charming cottage landscape containing plants with names like apothecary's rose, carpenter's weed, dittany of Crete, ground apple, lad's love, lark's heel, lamb's ears, silver king, and sweet balm?

Since I was a child, I have been fascinated with both gardening and cooking. Herbs just naturally fit into my lifestyle from the very beginning. I became enchanted by these ancient plants and have been using them for quite some time to embellish my garden and decorate my home. I enjoy using them in everything from culinary endeavors to homemade cosmetics and decorations. I am constantly amazed by how much these plants have to offer.

When I walk through an herb garden, I am constantly touching and smelling the plants to see which ones are the most fragrant. Lemon verbena, with its bright green leaves, has a very striking, lemon peel scent that lingers for hours. A small sprig of this herb can be rubbed on the skin to create an instant cologne! Chamomile (aka ground apple) has a sweet green-apple fragrance that is released whenever the foliage is bruised or stepped upon. I grow it between stepping stones leading to my herb garden so that visitors will have fragrance even before they reach the herbs themselves. Rosemary, with its rich, pine-like scent, has long been considered the symbol for remembrance, and I sometimes place a sprig of this herb inside a card or letter so that the fragrance will remind friends of their last visit.

All herbs have something to offer. Their usefulness in and around the home is truly unlimited. In this book, I explore many ways to preserve the flavors, capture the scents, and showcase the beauty of these wonderful plants. You will learn how herbs can be grown in the garden, utilized in the kitchen, and added to the home in a decorative manner. I hope you will use these ideas and develop a few of your own, because herbs are meant to be celebrated!

What Is an Herb?

That is a question that has plagued herbalists, historians, and garden writers for a long time. Hundreds of years ago, the answer was easier. Herbs were medicines and "pot herbs" were flavorings and vegetables. But today, the term "herb" encompasses more than just a plant with medicinal value.

By one definition, herbs are herbaceous plants that do not develop persistent woody stems. But if that were true, how would lavender, rosemary, and thyme be classified? Another definition states that an herb is a plant whose leaves, stems, roots, or flowers are used for their culinary, cosmetic, aromatic, and/or medicinal properties. This seems to be the most popular definition today and is the one used for this book. But even it has some problems. By that definition, most vegetables could be included as herbs also!

And what about spices? Some say that spices are the seeds, roots, or barks of woody plants that are native to the tropics. But where does that leave a plant like *Coriandrum sativum?* The seed of this plant is called "coriander" and is used as a spice. However, the foliage, called cilantro, is used as an herb!

Clearly, there are no easy, black-and-white answers. Herbs are many things to many people. It really doesn't matter how or why a plant is considered an herb or a spice. What is important is the usefulness, history, and charm of these valuable plants.

Herbs in the Garden

Having your own herb garden can be a wonderful adventure for the senses and will allow you to experience herbs firsthand. With the snip of your clippers, you'll have an endless variety of flavor combinations to be added to your next meal. You'll discover that colorful blossoms from herbs such as borage, nasturtium and calendula are just as comfortable and beautiful in your dinner salad as they are in a vase. As you touch, clip, or tread upon some of these extremely fragrant plants, you'll release the lovely perfume of their essential oils. You'll experience the spicy scent of sweet basil and the romantic fragrances of lavender and rose-scented geranium.

In order to fully enjoy these wonderful plants, you will definitely want to grow some yourself! If you don't already have an herb garden, Chapter 1, "35 Herbs to Grow," gives you a head start toward an herbal green thumb. It covers all the growing information you need. Even if you already have an herb garden, you will find many interesting bits of herbal history, lore, and uses in this chapter. As you read through the herb profiles, be sure to keep in mind that you don't have to have a large garden area in order to enjoy the advantages of home grown herbs. Chapter 2, "Getting Started," details how you can grow herbs just about anywhere! In Chapter 3, "The Basics," you will learn how to keep your garden healthy and happy once it's established.

Chapter 1

❦

35 Herbs to Grow

BOTANICAL NAMES

Although the Latin or botanical names of a plant can be hard to remember and difficult to pronounce, they are extremely important in distinguishing one herb from another. Common names vary from region to region and can be used to identify several different plants. Some plants have many relatives which all go by the same common name. For example, the name "oregano" has come to mean many different plants. Some have wonderful culinary flavors and others either taste rancid or have no flavor at all! As you can see, it would be very important to a cook to grow and use the culinary variety of oregano. Without botanical names, the task of finding the correct oregano would be tedious at best. That is why I have included the botanical names of each herb mentioned in this chapter. It should help you identify the precise species you are interested in growing and using.

Sometimes, a plant has been renamed (or reclassified) recently. The old botanical name may appear in some seed catalogs and older herbals. This can cause some confusion. Where known, I have included some of the other names a particular variety may be listed under.

ANNUALS/BIENNIALS/PERENNIALS

You will notice that each herb is classified as either an annual, a biennial, a perennial, or a tender perennial. An annual is a plant that completes an entire life cycle in one year. It grows, flowers, sets seed, and dies. It must be replanted each spring. A biennial will usually flourish the first season, but will set seed and die during the second year. A perennial is a plant that should come back each year and can usually survive freezing temperatures. A tender perennial is a plant that will survive year after year only if it is brought indoors during the cold winter months. It will not survive freezing temperatures. If it does not survive, it must be replanted in the spring, just like an annual.

There are many herbs to grow and use. But these 35 herbs should provide a good beginning for any herb enthusiast. Every herb listed is used several times throughout the book in recipes, crafts, and fragrances.

Herb Profiles

Aloe Vera
Aloe barbadensis and *Aloe vera*

TENDER PERENNIAL

Description: Aloe vera plants look very tropical with their long, tapering leaves. These leaves are filled with a mucilaginous gel that soothes, heals, and moisturizes the skin. It is recorded in history as being used over 2,000 years ago as a healing herb for wounds. Even Cleopatra is believed to have rubbed fresh aloe gel on her skin every day to stay young-looking.

Originally from South Africa, aloe vera must be wintered indoors in areas with frost. But this is not a problem if aloe is kept in pots all year round. It only grows to 2 feet tall and does very well in containers, as long as it is not overwatered. Outdoors, it prefers full sun, but will tolerate some light shade. Propagate by severing the small offshoots it produces during the growing season and replanting them. (You will find aloe listed under two different botanical names: *Aloe barbadensis* and *Aloe vera.*)

Uses: The thick gel in the leaves is very soothing on any type of burn, chapped skin, insect bites, and poison ivy. Simply cut off a piece of the leaf and open it up to reveal the gel inside. Then, gently rub this gel on the affected area. Owing to its healing properties, aloe vera is a very common ingredient in cosmetics for dry, sensitive skin.

Recommended:
Aloe vera *(Aloe barbadensis)*

Artemisia
Artemisia spp.
TENDER PERENNIAL

Description: There are over 300 artemisias, but only a handful are popular in American herb gardens. The few described here have long medicinal histories, but today are primarily grown in home gardens for their ornamental and fragrant foliage.

Wormwood *(Artemisia absinthium)* was once hung on doors to keep away evil spirits. It was also used as a strewing herb, insect repellant, and liqueur flavoring. It is still used to flavor vermouth.

Wormwood is a beautiful plant with finely divided, silvery-gray leaves. In the mornings, the foliage can be covered with sparkling dew drops, which give it a surreal look. It stands about 3-4 feet tall and can grow in full sun to partial shade. Unfortunately, wormwood does not make a good companion plant. It contains a substance called absinthin, which washes off the leaves into the soil. It is toxic to other plants and can inhibit their growth if they are planted within 2 feet. But outside of this 2-3-feet perimeter, your plants will do fine. Therefore, it is best to give wormwood plenty of space or a special section of its own. It also does very well in containers. Propagate by root division or cuttings.

> *While Wormwood hath seed get a handful or twaine,*
> *To save against March, to make flea to refraine;*
> *Where chamber is sweeped and Wormwood is strowne*
> *no flea for his life dar abide to be known.*
> *What savour is better (if physic be true)*
> *For places infected than Wormwood and Rue?"*
>
> —Thomas Tusser, Five Hundred Points, 1577

Southernwood *(A. abrotanum)* is also known as lover's plant, lad's love, and old man. It has feathery, gray-green foliage and stands about 3 feet tall. The leaves smell and taste bitter with a hint of lemon. The love-related names come from the old practice of putting sprigs into posies, which were then given to sweethearts. Southernwood was also used in aphrodisiac charms and perfumes. Like many other artemisias, southernwood is known for its insect-repelling qualities. Propagate by cuttings and layering.

Silver King Artemisia (*A. ludoviciana* 'Silver King') and Silver Queen Artemisia (*A. ludoviciana* 'Silver Queen') are grown in the same manner as the other artemisias. Both grow to 3 feet and are excellent wreath and craft herbs. Silver King has silvery, jagged leaves. Silver Queen has wider leaves and is more gray than silver. They are often confused for each other. (They are sometimes listed as *A. albula* 'Silver King' or 'Silver Queen'.)

Uses: All the abovementioned artemisias are so bitter tasting, they are seldom used in cooking. They are mainly grown for decorative and craft purposes. The leaves can be used in moth-repellant potpourri or hung in doorways and windows to repel flies. Their leaves are said to also repel beetles and mosquitos. Hang bundles wherever insects can be a problem.

The foliage of these plants is very useful in flower arranging. It can act as a filler or background to show off special flowers. Artemisias are also excellent for wreath and garland making. They hold their silver-green color well when dried.

Note: One artemisia *is* used extensively for cooking—*A. dracunculus,* better known as "French tarragon." *See* "Tarragon" in this chapter for more information.

Recommended:
Wormwood *(A. absinthium)*
Roman wormwood *(A. pontica)*
Southernwood *(A. abrotanum)*
Silver King *(A. lodoviciana* 'Silver King')

Basil
Ocimum basilicum

ANNUAL

Description: Common basil, aka sweet basil, has strongly scented green leaves and white flowers. Native to Asia, Africa, and South and Central Americas, basil is probably most associated with Italian cooking. Basil did not reach Britain until the sixteenth century and then it was carried to North America with the early settlers.

There are over 150 different varieties of basil with very diverse flavors and leaf structures. (A few of the most popular varieties are listed below.) They all prefer full sun and are easily propagated by seed. Sow the seeds directly outdoors or into pots. Basil seedlings have long tap roots and do not like to be transplanted. Basil plants grow very well in pots outdoors or on a sunny windowsill.

In warm weather, basil tends to bolt and set seed. Once the plant has set seed, it begins to die. To prolong the growing season, constantly pinch back the flower heads and use the flavorful flowers in cooking. They can be sprinkled over salad, sliced tomatoes, spaghetti, or soup.

Uses: Basil is most commonly known as a culinary herb because of its rich, spicy flavor. It is the main ingredient in Italian pesto sauce and is a staple in all tomato sauces. Basil is usually considered a savory herb, but it can be a valuable ingredient in some sweet dishes as well.

Fresh basil has a very delicate flavor which will dissipate with long cooking times. It is best to add the herb at the end of the cooking process. (If you are making a sauce and wish to flavor it slowly, you should used dried basil.) Fresh basil should be chopped at the last minute or it will turn brown. Common basil can also be used as a mosquito repellent.

Recommended:
Common basil *(Ocimum basilicum)*
Opal or purple basil *(O. basilicum* 'Purpurascens')
Lemon basil *(O. basilicum* 'Citriodora')
Cinnamon basil *(O. basilicum* 'Cinnamon')
Green ruffles basil *(O. basilicum* 'Green Ruffles')
Bush basil *(O. basilicum* 'Minimum')

Bay, Sweet
Laurus nobilis

TENDER PERENNIAL

© Copyright Wheeler Arts

Description: Sweet bay is also known as bay laurel. It is an evergreen, Mediterranean tree with glossy, dark green leaves. Bay is known throughout history as the symbol of glory, victory, and honor. The Greeks and Romans anointed the heads of athletes and soldiers with wreaths made of bay.

Bay has an interesting history in Greek mythology. According to legend, the Greek Sun God, Apollo, was madly in love with a nymph named Daphne. Unfortunately, Daphne wasn't interested in Apollo at all. To hide herself from Apollo, Daphne changed into a bay tree. Apollo declared the bay tree sacred. From that day forward, Apollo wore a wreath of bay on his head in Daphne's memory.

Bay has many preservative and antiseptic qualities. Throughout history, the smoke from burning bay leaves was believed to protect against infection. It was commonly used during plagues. It is probably for this reason that bay has the reputation of being protective against all kinds of things, including witchcraft, evil, and lightning.

In mild climates, such as in Southern California, the bay tree can grow as tall as 20 feet. But normally, it is a very slow grower and rarely grows over 4 feet. It is an excellent container plant and is commonly grown as a topiary. Bay is difficult to grow from seed. Propagate from cuttings or layering. Although this perennial will survive frost in many areas, the leaves can get damaged. It is better to bring the plant inside during the harsh winter months. Grow bay in full sun.

Uses: Bay is a common flavoring in all kinds of cuisines. It can be used to season soup, stew, pickles, sauce, shellfish, game, and beef. It is sometimes used to infuse the milk of both sweet and savory puddings and sauces. The leaves of the bay tree hold their color very well when dried. They can be used in potpourri, wreaths, and other crafts.

Recommended:
Sweet bay *(Laurus nobilis)*

Borage
Borago officinalis
ANNUAL

Description: Borage has a reputation for inducing courage and cheerfulness in those who partake in borage-flavored drinks (especially borage-flavored wine). Ancient Celtic warriors drank borage wine before going into battle. But no one knows for sure if it was the borage or the wine which eliminated their fears.

Borage is a highly ornamental plant that grows in full sun to 1 1/2–3 feet tall. Its leaves and stems are covered with tiny, stiff hairs. In midsummer, this herb is covered with bright blue, star-shaped flowers. The beautiful flowers have distinctive black anthers and are a favorite among the bees. Although borage is an annual, it usually self-seeds and comes up in the same area each spring. Borage grows quite easily from seed, but it has a long tap root and does not like to be transplanted. Sow seed directly in the garden in midspring.

Uses: Historically, borage has been used as a diuretic. More recently, the oil produced from borage seed has been found to contain high amounts of gamma linolenic acid (GLA) which has become a popular dietary supplement. Unfortunately, borage oil is very expensive because the seeds are extremely difficult to collect for processing. Some sources suggest that borage leaves and flowers should not be taken internally in large quantities or for long periods of time. However occasional consumption of young leaves and flowers pose no problems.

The young leaves have a cucumber flavor and can be used raw, steamed, or sautéed. They do not hold their flavor when dried or frozen, so they should only be used fresh. The flowers are commonly used to garnish candies, drinks, salads, and cakes. Borage is very ornamental and makes an unusual specimen plant. That alone makes it a good choice for any herb garden.

Recommended:
Borage *(Borago officinalis)*

Burnet, Salad

Poterium sanguisorba

PERENNIAL

© Copyright Theresa Loe

Description: Salad burnet was very popular in Elizabethan England and was later a prevalent landscape plant in English cottage gardens. The Colonists brought burnet to America, where it is still treasured for its flavor and textured foliage. This delicate-looking herb has slender stems and dainty, fern-like leaves which have a distinctive cucumber flavor. (In the summer heat, the taste may change to sweet watermelon.) In midsummer it produces red-tipped, sphere-shaped flowers. It is commonly called burnet, salad burnet, or garden burnet. You may find it classified in older herb books as *Sanguisorba minor.* Today it is given the botanical name *Poterium sanguisorba.*

Salad burnet prefers full sun, but can tolerate partial shade. It is generally evergreen and can withstand most winters. It can be propagated by division or seeds. In fact, the plant is known to re-seed itself so well, it can become a slight nuisance.

Uses: Due to its delicious cucumber flavor, burnet is a popular salad herb. But it can also be added to salad dressings, cold soups, soft cheeses, delicate sauces, vegetable dishes, and chicken and fish recipes. It makes an excellent herb vinegar, which can be used for dressings and marinades. The leaves contain vitamin C and should be picked from the center of the plant, while young. The older leaves can be tough and bitter.

The leaves of salad burnet do not hold their flavor when dried. Therefore, only fresh leaves are recommended for culinary purposes.

Recommended:
Salad burnet *(Poterium sanguisorba)*

Calendula
Calendula officinalis

HARDY ANNUAL

Description: Ancient herbalists called them marigolds. Today they are known by their botanical name, calendula, or their common name, pot marigold. Not to be confused with other marigolds (which are members of the genus *Tagetes*), calendulas are popular and useful bedding plants. They have oblong leaves with fine hairs and cheerful flowers, which range in color from pale yellow to deep orange. They flower almost continuously from early summer to late fall. Deadheading the spent flowers helps promote more blooms.

Grown for centuries in cottage gardens, calendulas are still popular as border and edging plants. They grow in neat, compact clumps which are about 1–2 feet tall. They prefer full sun, but in areas with very hot summers, they prefer some partial shade. They are easily propagated from fresh seed.

Calendulas are susceptible to powdery mildew and leaf spot, so they should be grown where there is good air circulation and drainage. They are sometimes attacked by leafhoppers, aphids, or whitefly. If this happens, dislodge the critters with a strong spray of water or use insecticidal soap for control.

Uses: Calendulas are most commonly used in culinary dishes. Sometimes called the poor man's saffron, the flowers can be dried and ground into a saffron substitute. They are added fresh to salads, sandwiches, soups, custards, butters, vegetables, rice, and cheese. They make excellent herbal vinegar and can be used as a festive garnish on just about anything.

Calendulas are said to have astringent, antiseptic, antifungal, and anti-inflammatory properties—which is probably why they are commonly used in commercial and homemade cosmetics. Calendula flowers have many ornamental uses as well. They can be used in fresh and dried flower arrangements. The dried petals make a colorful addition to potpourri too.

To use the fresh calendula blossoms, pick the flowers to use whole, or remove the individual petals. For dried petals, let the entire calendula blossom dry before removing the individual petals. The dried petals hold their color well and should be stored in an airtight container.

Recommended:
Pot marigold *(Calendula officinalis)*

Chamomile
Chamaemelum nobile
PERENNIAL

Description: *Chamaemelum nobile* (formerly known as *Anthemis nobilis*) is commonly called Roman or English chamomile.

There is some controversy about which *Chamaemelum* species is "the true" chamomile. But in most English-speaking countries, the perennial Roman chamomile is considered "true" chamomile. It grows to only about 8 inches tall when flowering and it has delicious apple-scented, feathery foliage. The flowers are small, daisy-like blossoms which stand on thin stems.

Another plant, with very similar characteristics, is also known as chamomile. Its botanic name is *Matricaria recutita* and its common name is German chamomile. German chamomile looks almost exactly like Roman chamomile except it grows taller and is an annual rather than a perennial. (The fragrance of Roman chamomile is a bit stronger.)

The name "chamomile" means "ground apple," and Roman chamomile makes an excellent ground cover, which releases the apple fragrance when stepped upon. Grow it between stepping stones or as a chamomile lawn. It prefers full sun to partial shade and does not do well in extreme heat. Southern gardeners may have to grow it as an annual. Propagate by division or seed. (The seeds should not be covered with soil because they need light to germinate.)

Uses: Chamomile has a long history as an herbal remedy, dating back to ancient Egypt and Greece. Even Peter Rabbit's mother knew the value of chamomile tea! Tea is made from dried chamomile blossoms and is used to aid indigestion and act as a mild sedative. And save those tea bags! Chamomile has anti-inflammatory properties, which make the tea bags excellent compresses for puffy eyes.

Chamomile is also a popular cosmetic ingredient. It is used in hair rinses to accentuate natural blond highlights and in lotions or creams to soothe and soften skin. The apple scent makes a nice addition to potpourri and flower arrangements as well.

Recommended:
Roman chamomile *(Chamaemelum nobile)*

Chives

Allium schoenoprasum

PERENNIAL

© Copyright Wheeler Arts

Description: There are over 400 species in the allium family including chives, garlic, leeks, and onions. The chive plant *(Allium schoenoprasum)* is the smallest member of this onion family and is sometimes called "onion chives." Owing to their beauty and versatility, chives are very popular in American herb gardens. They have dark green, reed-like leaves which are hollow and stand about 8–12 inches tall. They grow in clumps resembling small tufts of grass and have round, purple-pink blossoms that are actually made up of many tiny flowers. Chives grow in full to partial sun.

Onion chives are easy to grow from seed or division and do very well in pots and window boxes. They should be divided every 3–4 years. The leaves should be snipped from the base of the plant to encourage regrowth. They have a sweet, mild onion taste and are high in vitamins A and C.

There is another variety of chive called garlic or Chinese chives *(A. tuberosum)*, which is useful to grow. It resembles onion chives but has flat (rather than hollow) leaves and white blossoms. The flavor of this slightly larger plant is similar to mild garlic and can actually be substituted for garlic in cooking. Garlic chives are slightly less vigorous than onion chives.

Uses: Onion chives are very popular in both American and French cooking. They are generally used fresh because they do not dry well at home. (The commercially dried chives found in the store are freeze-dried.) Chives should be added at the end of recipes, because long cooking times can dissipate their flavor. Use scissors or a very sharp knife to mince or chop the chives. A dull knife can pulverize them! Fresh chives can be added to salads, vegetables, cheese, butter, eggs, sauces, or chicken and fish recipes. The leaves are sometimes tied decoratively around julienned vegetables. The flowers are also flavorful in the abovementioned recipes and can add color to flower arrangements.

Recommended:
Onion chives *(Allium schoenoprasum)*
Garlic chives *(A. tuberosum)*

Coriander/Cilantro
Coriandrum sativum

ANNUAL

Description: This herb has an ancient history as a culinary herb and has been grown for thousands of years in India and China. It was popular in England up to the Tudor Era. The Colonists brought seed over from England to America. It is one of the few herbs which has a different name for the seed and the leaves of the same plant. The seeds of the plant are generally called coriander seeds. But when referring to the foliage, this plant is called cilantro or Chinese parsley. Although this can be confusing, all three names are correct.

Coriander/cilantro grows in full sun and has very strong smelling and tasting foliage. The lower leaves are fan-like and look very similar to Italian flat-leaf parsley. The upper leaves are lacy and feathery, like dill. This herb has delicate, pinkish-white flowers which appear in umbrella-shaped clusters. The delicate flower stems can snap in the wind, so some staking or protection may be necessary. If you live in an area with extremely hot summers, you may want to plant this herb in partial shade and keep it watered well.

Coriander/cilantro is very easy to grow from seed and it self-sows freely. It has a long tap root which makes it difficult to transplant, so you should sow the seeds directly in the garden or pots. Harvest the seeds in mid- to late summer right as they ripen. If you wait too long, they will fall off in the garden and scatter. This herb does very well in pots, but is not recommended for indoor growing owing to its strong fragrance. It grows to about 12–18 inches tall and makes a pretty border plant.

Uses: Many people do not care for the flavor or scent of cilantro leaves. Some claim it is an acquired taste. However, in the Southwestern United States, cilantro is as common as parsley in restaurants and grocery stores. It is used in Mexican, Chinese, and Vietnamese dishes. The leaves can be added to rice, chutneys, beans, and spicy sauces. It blends very well with tomato or lime flavorings. When using cilantro for the first time, use a very light hand. The flavor can easily overpower the dish. Cilantro is a delicate herb and should be added at the end of cooking or sprinkled raw over the dish.

Coriander seed is more familiar to people. The seed is popular in pastries, breads, pickles, and curries.

Recommended:
Coriander/cilantro *(Coriandrum sativum)*

Dill
Anethum graveolens

ANNUAL

Description: Magicians and sorcerers used dill to cast spells. Old herbals boasted that it could cure hiccups. But dill is probably most noted for being a pickle herb (dill pickles). Growing in full sun, dill will reach a height of 2–4 feet. It has lacy blue-green foliage with large umbels of tiny yellow flowers. The flowers will produce brown, oval-shaped seeds. All parts are aromatic and flavorful, which is probably why dill has been so popular in herb gardens throughout history. Dill is very attractive to bees. Be careful not to disturb them when you are harvesting it.

Dill has a long tap root and does not transplant well. It should be propagated by seeds which are planted directly in the garden. They should only be lightly covered with soil because they need some light to germinate. For a continuous supply of seeds and leaves, dill should be planted in successive plantings from spring to midsummer. It is sensitive to wind damage and should be placed in the garden where it will receive some protection. The seeds should be harvested when the tips begin to turn light brown. (*See* "Harvesting and Drying Herbs" in Chapter 2 for more information.)

Uses: Dill has many other uses besides being the main flavoring in dill pickles. It can be added to potato salad, herb butter, bread, dip, cheese, vegetables, eggs, and fish recipes. It makes an excellent vinegar, which can be used to create salad dressings and marinades. The foliage has a lighter taste than the seeds and is called "dill weed" in many recipes. Snip some fresh dill leaves and toss them into foods at the end of the cooking time. Dill is delicate and cannot stand high heat for long periods of time.

The seeds are said to aid in digestion and have a calming, sedative effect. They can be chewed to freshen the breath. The flower umbels make excellent additions to flower arrangements, because their unusual shape adds a touch of lightness.

Recommended:
Dill *(Anethum graveolens)*

Fennel
Foeniculum vulgare

PERENNIAL

Description: Common fennel grows from 3 to 5 feet, depending upon the climate, and has filigreed leaves and umbels of flowers. It looks very similar to dill. It is said that dill and fennel should not be planted next to each other in the garden or they might cross-pollinate. Fennel has a very distinctive anise or licorice flavor and is much loved by bees and butterflies. It grows in full sun and is best propagated by seed which is sown directly into the garden.

There are also several annual varieties of fennel. The most popular for culinary purposes is Florence fennel *(Foeniculum vulgare* var. *azoricum)*. It has a shorter bulb and is also known as finocchio, sweet anise, or vegetable fennel. It is often confused with another annual, *F. vulgare* var. *dulce,* which has thinner leaves at the base. Both can be used in cooking.

SWALLOWTAIL BUTTERFLIES

Fennel plants are hosts to many swallowtail butterfly species. They might spend their entire lives living on or near a fennel plant. The colorful caterpillars have beautiful markings and will not overly damage the plant. If you find one, leave it alone and soon you may find its chrysalis hanging from a stem. In no time at all, a beautiful swallowtail butterfly will emerge and flutter around your garden!

Uses: All parts of the fennel plant are edible and delicious. The seeds are commonly used in cakes, breads, cookies, sausage, liqueurs, butters, and fish recipes. The stalk, bulb, and leaves can be used to flavor salads, vegetables, rice, cheese, soup, and chicken and fish recipes. The Florence fennel bulb is commonly used as a vegetable. It can be steamed or sautéed with other root vegetables to create a delicious side dish.

The seeds are sometimes used to soothe a hungry stomach and to sweeten the breath. Mild fennel tea is sometimes consumed by nursing mothers to help relieve their baby's colic. Fennel is also used to dye wool a pretty yellow or brown color. The leaves are said to be astringent and are sometimes used in cosmetic recipes.

Recommended:
Common fennel *(Foeniculum vulgare)*
Florence fennel *(F. vulgare* var. *azoricum):* Annual.
Bronze leaf fennel *(F. vulgare* 'Rubrum'): This fennel has beautiful, coppery foliage.

Feverfew
Chrysanthemum parthenium

PERENNIAL

*"... Of joys that come to womankind
The loom of fate doth weave her few,
But here are summer joys entwined
And bound with golden feverfew."*

—GEORGE R. SIMS (1847–1922)

Description: Feverfew is a semi-evergreen perennial which grows in full sun to partial shade. It has divided yellow-green leaves and small, white, daisy-like flowers. There are both single- and double-blooming varieties.

Feverfew is easy to grow from seeds, division, or cuttings. The seeds should not be covered with soil when planting because they need light to germinate. To grow feverfew as a perennial, you must pinch off the flowers before they go to seed. If you don't, the plant may die after setting seed. However, if the flowers are removed, feverfew will stay bushy and continue to grow for another season. In some areas, feverfew is grown as a half-hardy annual. (Feverfew is sometimes listed as *Tanacetum parthenium.)*

Uses: Feverfew was once used as a cure for fevers (hence, the name). But today, it is more commonly thought of as a possible headache remedy. There are many studies being conducted on the benefits of eating feverfew leaves to cure migraines and arthritis pain. One problem with feverfew is that some people are allergic to it and many people get irritating sores in their mouths from eating it.

Feverfew should be grown for its many ornamental and decorative qualities. It is a lovely cottage garden plant and is very attractive in window boxes and perennial borders. It is an excellent flower arrangement plant because the flowers can hold up both in and out of water. When dried, feverfew is terrific in all kinds of craft projects.

Recommended:
Double flowering feverfew (*Tanacetum parthenium* 'Flore Pleno')
Golden feverfew (*T. parthenium* var. *aureum*): Light yellow-green leaves that are extremely ornamental in the garden and in craft projects.

Hyssop
Hyssopus officinalis
PERENNIAL

Description: Hyssop is a very beautiful, semi-evergreen shrub with bushy growth and narrow, aromatic leaves. Its flowers are very attractive to bees, butterflies, and humans! From June to late August, hyssop has spiked branches that are covered with whorls of deep blue blossoms. There are also pink and white blooming varieties. Bees are so attracted to this plant, that beekeepers used to rub the hives with hyssop leaves to keep the bees nearby. When bees frequently visit hyssop flowers, their honey develops a delicious flavor. Elizabethans loved to grow hyssop as a hedge in their knot gardens. The only disadvantage to a hyssop hedge is that the constant pruning never allows the plant to come into full flower.

Hyssop has a long history of being used as a cleaning and purifying herb. It was strewn over sickroom floors and used in the purifying rituals of temples. A distilled oil of hyssop has been used in perfumery for centuries and is mentioned in many of the old recipes for *eau-de-Cologne*. It was also used in soap recipes and as a flavoring for liqueur.

Hyssop grows to about 1–2 feet tall in full sun. It will accept some light shade. The leaves have a camphor-like odor, which may explain why it is seldom bothered by pests or disease. Hyssop can be propagated by seeds, cuttings, and division. The seeds are slow to germinate so they should be sown in early spring.

Uses: Hyssop's leaves have a bitter, slightly mint flavor. They can be used in salad, rice, cheese, and lamb or chicken recipes. But hyssop is probably most valued for its ornamental qualities. It not only is very colorful in the garden, but is an excellent flower-arranging herb. The dried flowers and leaves can be added to pot-pourri too.

Recommended:
Hyssop *(Hyssopus officinalis)*
White blooming hyssop *(H. officinalis* 'Alba')
Pink blooming hyssop *(H. officinalis* 'Rosea')

Lamb's Ears
Stachys byzantina
PERENNIAL

© Copyright Theresa Loe

Description: Lamb's ears (aka woolly betony and woundwort) has dense, woolen, silver-gray foliage. Each fuzzy leaf feels exactly like a soft lamb or bunny ear. The plant forms a spectacular carpet in the garden with silver rosettes of leaves that stand approximately 8 inches tall. The pink flowers form on thick, fuzzy stems that are 1–2 feet tall. Lamb's ears have an endearing quality. Everyone seems to love them, especially children. Once they touch the soft leaves, people just can't seem to stop petting them. Hummingbirds and bees are especially attracted to the blossoms of this ornamental plant.

Lamb's ears can be propagated by seeds or division. People in highly humid areas may have difficulty growing this herb. It does not do well with excessive moisture of any kind. It is extremely ornamental and makes an attractive specimen when grown under rosebushes. It is also perfect for a silver garden or a moon garden when combined with white blooming plants.

Uses: The leaves of lamb's ears are mildly astringent, and in the past, they were used to bandage wounds. The leaves have an absorbing quality, which helped stop mild bleeding. However, today this plant is grown purely as an ornamental. The gray foliage and fuzzy-stemmed blossoms are particularly attractive in fresh-cut flower arrangements because of their unusual texture. The Victorians used lamb's ears extensively in posies. The fresh leaves can be used to cover an entire wreath and then allowed to dry in place. The leaves hold their gray color very well when dried.

Recommended:
Lamb's ears *(Stachys byzantina)*

Lavender
Lavandula angustifolia
TENDER PERENNIAL

© Copyright Wheeler Arts

"And Lavender, whose spikes of azure bloom
Shall be erewhile, in arid bundles bound,
To lurk amidst her labours of the loom,
And crown her kerchiefs clean with mickle rare
perfume."

—WILLIAM SHENSTONE

Description: There are many different species and varieties to choose from, but English lavender *(Lavandula angustifolia)* is probably one of the most well known. (It is sometimes listed as *L. vera.*) It grows in full sun to a height of 2–3 feet. It is a bushy shrub with gray-green leaves and purple spike flowers. (There are also white and pink blooming varieties available.)

Lavender can be propagated by seeds. However, cuttings or layering is recommended to ensure that the offspring is true to the mother plant. It makes a great potted plant and can even be trained into a topiary or bonsai shape. Lavender is traditionally planted in cottage gardens, along walkways, and in rock gardens. If planted outside a window, the sweet fragrance can waft in with a gentle breeze. In areas with cold winters, lavender should be potted up and brought indoors for the winter. Lavender does not tolerate humidity well.

Valued for centuries for its beauty, fragrance, flavor, and cosmetic properties, lavender has become a classic in the herb garden. The name *Lavandula* comes from the Latin *lavare,* which means "to wash." A standard ingredient in soaps, lavender has a long history as a cleaning and purifying herb. Linen was often dried on the blooming bushes of lavender to impart its fragrance. Lavender was also believed to protect against everything from witchcraft to the evil eye. Victorians believed that the fragrance was so powerful, they even used it in their smelling salts to revive swooning women.

Uses: Although lavender has gone out of fashion as a flavoring, it has a deliciously sweet flavor that should be more utilized. It can be used in jelly, custards, ice cream, cookies, and various other desserts and pastries.

Lavender is probably best known for its fragrant and cosmetic properties. It can be used to make soaps, toilet waters, perfumes, lotions, and many other aromatic cosmetics. The romance of lavender can also be captured in potpourri, sachets, and sleep pillows. Dried lavender is known for its moth-repelling virtues and makes a very refreshing alternative to moth balls. The blossoms of lavender hold their fragrance and color very well and should be used freely in dried crafts.

Recommended:
English lavender *(Lavandula angustifolia)*
Hidcote lavender *(L. angustifolia* 'Hidcote')
French lavender *(L. dentata)*
Pink blooming lavender *(L. angustifolia* 'Rosea')

Lemon Balm
Melissa officinalis

TENDER PERENNIAL

© Copyright Linda Chlup

Description: Lemon balm is also known as balm, sweet balm, and melissa. It is a loosely branched plant with lemon-scented and -flavored foliage. It reached its peak in popularity during the Elizabethan Era, where it was used to flavor food, wine, and tea. It was brought to America with the Colonists and was used as a tea to relieve melancholy. (Thomas Jefferson even grew lemon balm at Monticello.) Its lovely, lemon scent made it useful as a strewing herb and its leaves were rubbed on furniture to make the wood sweet-smelling. But lemon balm is probably best known throughout history as a bee herb. It was rubbed inside the bee hives to encourage bees to move in. It was also believed that the fragrance calmed the bees. In fact, "Melissa" is the Greek name for honey-bee.

The leaves of lemon balm are light green and oval-shaped with scalloped edges. The flowers are tiny, white, and inconspicuous. Lemon balm grows to approximately 2 feet in full sun, but it will tolerate some shade. (In very hot climates, it prefers it.) It can be propagated by seeds, layering, or division. For quick propagation, division is the best choice. The seeds will germinate best if they are left uncovered. Although lemon balm is related to mint, it is much better behaved in the garden than ordinary mint. The roots spread but are easily torn out, which makes the plant very con-trollable. Lemon balm is deciduous. It should be mulched in cold areas through the winter to protect the roots.

Uses: Lemon balm has many culinary uses. It can be added to fruit desserts, ice cream, custards, and pastries. It can be used to make tea, punch, flavored liqueur, or extra tangy lemonade. The leaves are best when fresh and can be used to season chicken, fish, and vegetables. You can be generous when cooking with lemon balm because the leaves have a delicate flavor.

The fresh foliage is terrific in flower arrangements and the dried leaves can be used to create lemon-scented potpourri.

Recommended:
Common lemon balm (*Melissa officinalis*)
Golden lemon balm (*M. officinalis* 'Aurea')
Variegated lemon balm (*M. officinalis* 'Variegata')

Lemon Grass
Cymbopogon citratus

TENDER PERENNIAL

Description: Lemon grass is a tropical plant and only grows well outside in the Southern or West Coast regions of the United States. It grows in large clumps with long, narrow, grass-like leaves and it rarely flowers. It can reach a height of 6 feet in some climates but generally stands 3–4 feet tall. The bright green, bulbous stems and leaves have a very strong lemon scent and flavor. It makes a very nice specimen plant in the garden. It grows in full sun to partial shade and should be propagated by division. It will survive in areas with mild winters, but should be heavily mulched in areas reaching 20 degrees. Areas with colder winters should grow lemon grass as a potted herb and bring it indoors in the winter. It does very well in greenhouses.

Uses: Lemon grass is commonly used in Thai and Vietnamese cuisine. It can be used whole or chopped, but in either case, the leaves should be bruised to release the flavorful oils. It can be used to flavor steamed vegetables, rice, curries, chicken, and fish. It has antiseptic properties and is used in some cosmetics. Commercially, the oil is used as an artificial flavoring for lemon candies. The fragrance holds up well when dried, which makes lemon grass an excellent addition to citrus potpourri.

Recommended:
Lemon grass *(Cymbopogon citratus)*

Lemon Verbena
Aloysia triphylla

TENDER PERENNIAL

© Copyright Theresa Loe

Description: This strongly scented, woody shrub can reach a height of 10 feet, but generally stays about 4–5 feet in most areas. It has whorls of bright green leaves and spikes of pale, white flowers. It prefers full sun and is hardy only to about 20 degrees. In areas with cold winters, it must be potted up and brought indoors. It grows very well in containers, but should be fed regularly if grown year round as a potted plant. Keep in mind that lemon verbena is deciduous. Don't be alarmed if it loses all of its leaves in the winter. This extremely aromatic plant is best propagated from cuttings and is sometimes listed by its old name, *Lippia citriodora.*

Uses: Lemon verbena has always been a popular fragrance among women. Even today, the essential oil is used in some colognes. (In *Gone With the Wind,* lemon verbena was mentioned as the favorite cologne of Scarlet O'Hara's mother.) Fragrant infusions can be made from the leaves and used to scent bath waters. It can be used in many other cosmetic recipes as well.

The flavor of lemon verbena is very strong and lemony. It can be used in place of lemon juice in hot tea and iced drinks. It can be used as a flavoring in desserts, pastries, jellies, rice, and salad dressings. It is also a delicious seasoning in chicken and fish recipes. A tea brewed from its leaves is said to be mildly sedative.

Sprigs of this aromatic plant are exquisite in all types of fresh flower arrangements. They are so fragrant, they can be hung in a closet to freshen musty air. When dried, they can be added to potpourri recipes.

Recommended:
Lemon verbena *(Aloysia triphylla)*

Marjoram
Origanum majorana
TENDER PERENNIAL/HALF HARDY ANNUAL

Description: Sweet marjoram was believed to be a favorite herb of the goddess of love, Aphrodite. Wreaths of marjoram were worn by bridal couples in ancient Greece to sanctify marital bliss. Marjoram was also used as a strewing herb and was thought to impart disinfectant qualities when strewn in sickrooms. The leaves and oil have been used as a furniture polish for wooden floors, tables, and chairs.

There are many cultivated species of marjoram on the market. The best culinary marjoram is probably *Origanum majorana,* which is known as marjoram, sweet marjoram, or knotted marjoram. It is a Mediterranean herb that grows as a tender perennial in warm climates. In colder areas, it is grown as an annual. It prefers full sun and has small gray-green leaves. The white flowers are small and the seed clusters look like tiny knots. It reaches approximately 1–2 feet when flowering.

If you have difficulty growing sweet marjoram, you might want to try the hybrid *O.* x *majoricum.* It is a hybrid between *O. majorana* and *O. vulgare* var. *virens.* It is easier to cultivate and can be substituted for sweet marjoram in recipes.

For culinary purposes, do *not* try to use wild marjoram *(O. vul-*

gare subsp. *vulgare)*, which is sometimes erroneously sold as oregano. It looks like oregano, but has pinkish-purple flowers. Although it is excellent for flower arrangements and crafts, it does not have a good culinary flavor. (I grow wild marjoram in my cut flower garden.)

Sweet marjoram can be grown from seed but the seeds you buy are not always true. You may have better luck buying the actual plant from a reputable nursery or taking divisions from someone's garden. Marjoram can also be propagated by layering.

Uses: Sweet marjoram is sweeter than oregano and can be used in many of the same recipes. Try adding it to red meat, chicken, and vegetables. It can also be used in vinegar, marinades, herb butter, cheese, soup, and stuffing.

Marjoram is mildly antiseptic and is found in some cosmetic recipes. It is also very good in wreaths and flower arrangements.

Recommended:
Sweet marjoram *(O. majorana)*
Golden marjoram *(O. majorana* 'Aureum')
Marjoram hybrid *(O. x majoricum,)*

Mint

Mentha spp.

PERENNIAL

Description: Mint hybridizes very easily and there are literally hundreds of different varieties to choose from. Peppermint and spearmint are probably familiar to most people because they are used to flavor candy, gum, and toothpaste. But there are many other varieties worthy of a place in your herb garden. For example, you might want to grow apple mint *(Mentha suaveolens)* with its fuzzy, light green leaves and sweet apple fragrance. It can be used in fruit salads or as a garnish in ice tea. Another choice might be Corsican mint *(M. requienii)* with its tiny leaves and very potent fragrance. Unlike the other mints, Corsican mint prefers shade and grows in a mossy form just a few inches tall. If you want a plant with flea-repelling qualities, you should grow pennyroyal *(M. pulegium)*. It can be made into an infusion to rinse pets or strewn over bedding areas to deter fleas. It is also a moth repellant.

Almost all the mints prefer full sun (except Corsican mint) but can tolerate some shade. They generally grow 1–3 feet tall, depending upon the variety. You will read in gardening books that mint is a notorious spreader and can easily over take your entire garden. But don't let that deter you from growing it; it can be controlled. The plant spreads by root runners which travel either underground or across the topsoil. To prevent an invasion, you can sink barriers about 6 inches underground around the plants. You will still have to watch closely, though, because the runners can still travel over and around the barriers. Your second choice is to grow mint in containers. It does very well in pots, hanging baskets, and window boxes.

Mint is extremely easy to propagate by layering, divisions, or cuttings. Just about any little piece of mint that has a node can grow into a plant. (That is why it can get out of hand in the garden.)

Uses: Peppermint and spearmint have long histories as medicinal plants and they are still popular today. Peppermint tea helps relieve headaches, insomnia, and upset stomachs. Spearmint is often chewed to freshen the breath and is usually the more popular herb of choice in culinary dishes. Both herbs were used as strewing herbs. They were sprinkled on the floor of sickrooms and living areas to sweeten the air when stepped upon.

Mint can be used in both savory and sweet dishes. It is especially flavorful in tea, desserts, candy, cordials, jellies, and fruit recipes. It can also be used with lamb, duck, fish, and vegetables. (It is especially good with peas and carrots.) Mint is a classic flavoring with anything chocolate. Try using peppermint, spearmint, apple mint, and orange mint in your culinary adventures.

Mint is used in both homemade and commercial cosmetics and soaps. It is said to cool the skin in hot weather and soothe irritated, dry skin. It can also be used in sweet-smelling flower arrangements and potpourri.

Recommended:
Peppermint *(Mentha* x *piperita)*
Spearmint *(M. spicata)*
Apple mint *(M. suaveolens)*
Variegated apple mint *(M. s.* 'Variegata'): Also known as variegated pineapple mint.
Corsican mint *(M. requienii)*
Orange mint *(M.* x *piperita* var. *citrata)*
English pennyroyal *(M. pulegium* var. *erecta)*

Nasturtium

Tropaeolum majus

ANNUAL

Description: Nasturtiums (lovingly referred to as "nasties" by some) are native to South America and first came to Europe from Peru via Spanish explorers in the 1500s. Within a few years they reached England. They soon became popular in the garden and kitchen. Nasturtiums are lovely trailing plants with flat, round leaves and colorful, trumpet-shaped flowers. The flowers come in all shades of yellow, red, and orange. They are sometimes referred to as "lark's heel" in old herbals because "unto the backe-part (of the flowers) doth hang a taile or spurre, such as hath the Larkes heel" (Gerard).

You can find both climbing and dwarf forms of this plant as well as variegated varieties. You can grow nasties in hanging baskets, tubs, pots, window boxes, or directly in the garden. Unless you have a slope or large area you wish to cover with flowers, you should grow climbing forms on a trellis or fence. A south facing wall or slope is usually best. This plant is propagated by seed in early spring. It prefers full sun to partial shade and will bloom from summer until fall in most areas. Don't overfertilize the soil before planting nasturtiums. They do best in very poor soil. (Fertile soil produces lush growth and few flowers.)

Uses: All parts of the nasturtium are edible. The leaves were once used as a remedy for scurvy and are now known to be high in vitamin C and iron. They have a strong, peppery flavor. The flowers have a more subdued flavor. Use both to give a bite to savory foods. Add fresh leaves or flowers to salad, sandwiches, cheese, and dip. All parts can be used to make a peppery vinegar. For a pretty appetizer, the flowers can be stuffed with cheese.

Recommended:
Nasturtium *(Tropaeolum majus)*
Variegated *(T. majus* 'Alaska')
Dwarf hybrid *(T. majus nanum* 'Tom Thumb')

Oregano
Origanum vulgare subsp. *hirtum*
TENDER PERENNIAL

Description: There is much confusion as to which plants are true culinary oreganos and which are not. There are many different *Origanum* species with very similar physical attributes. But when it comes to flavor, there are only a few worthy of culinary uses. Greek oregano *(Origanum vulgare* subsp. *hirtum)* is considered by many to be "True" oregano. It is sometimes listed in plant catalogs as *O. hirtum* or *O. heracleoticum* and has white blossoms. Wild marjoram *(O. vulgare* subsp. *vulgare)* is sometimes sold as oregano but it has pink flowers and no flavor. It can become very confusing! You may even find seed and plant catalogs which list a certain plant as "oregano" but give the botanical name for "wild marjoram." If you are looking for an oregano for cooking, you should avoid wild marjoram or you will be very disappointed. Wild marjoram is better suited to flower arrangements.

Your best bet for getting Greek oregano is to order from a seed catalog that lists the correct botanical name or take a cutting from someone who has a flavorful white blooming variety. (Oregano can also be propagated by root division.) If you decide to try seeds, do not cover them with soil because they need light to germinate. Greek oregano has a peppery flavor and grows in full sun to a height of approximately 2 feet. It has round, green leaves with a pungent scent.

Keep in mind that there is more to life than just cooking and there are several beautiful varieties of oregano to try besides Greek oregano. You might want to grow dittany of Crete *(O. dictamnus)* with its small hop-like bracts and a cascading growth habit. It is gorgeous in a hanging basket! There is also a pretty variety called Golden Creeping Oregano (*O. vulgare* subsp. *vulgare* 'Aureum').

Most varieties do not do well in humid weather. They can usually survive mild winters with a heavy mulching, but in extremely cold winters, the plants should be potted up and brought indoors. Bees and butterflies love all the oreganos.

Uses: Oregano is most associated with Italian cooking and makes an excellent addition to anything with tomato sauce (spaghetti, pizza, etc.). It did not catch on as a culinary herb in America until about 1940. Now it is extremely popular in all kinds of meat and vegetable dishes. It can be used with beef, game, pork, eggs, and breads.

Oregano tea has been used to relieve coughs, headaches, and indigestion. Fresh leaves can be added to bath water to help relieve achy muscles. The flowers can be used in wreaths, flower arranging, and other crafts.

Recommended:
Greek oregano *(O. vulgare* subsp. *hirtum)*
Dittany of Crete *(O. dictamnus)*

Parsley

Petroselinum crispum

HARDY BIENNIAL

Description: Parsley is a very recognizable herb. Who hasn't seen a sprig of parsley lying on a plate in a restaurant? But parsley is much more than a garnish. It is indispensable in the kitchen and is quite beautiful in the garden.

There are two main varieties which are popular in America today: curly leaf parsley *(Petroselinum crispum)* and Italian flat-leaf parsley *(P. crispum* var. *neapolitanum)*. Both can be grown in full sun to partial shade and reach a height of 6–10 inches. When flowering, the clusters of greenish-yellow flowers can reach 2 1/2 feet. The leaves of parsley are triangular and deeply divided. Many people grow parsley as an annual, because when it flowers in the second year, the leaves are no longer useful in cooking. After flowering, the plant sets seed and dies.

Parsley is best propagated by seeds which are sown directly into the garden. It used to be believed that if parsley was trans-planted, misfortune would befall the household. I guess if you could call the death of your parsley plant "misfortune," then that statement is true. Parsley seedlings do not like to be transplanted and can go into shock or die if moved.

You have to be patient when growing parsley from seed. They can take up to 6 weeks to germinate. (There is an old saying that parsley seeds go to the Devil seven times before sprouting.) You can help speed up the process, by soaking the seeds overnight in water before planting.

Parsley likes to be grown in pots. It does very well in window boxes and can even be grown on a kitchen windowsill. Just be sure that the indoor plants receive at least 4–5 hours of sunlight per day.

Uses: Parsley is very high in vitamin C. It can be used generously in almost all savory recipes and tends to blend or enhance the other flavors. The Italian flat-leaf parsley has a slightly better flavor than curly leaf parsley and is usually the parsley of choice among chefs. The stems and leaves can be added to salads, soups, eggs, vegetables, rice, bread, and meat dishes. It can also be used to create delicious sauces and herbal butters.

Parsley is high in chlorophyl, which can act as a natural breath freshener. That's why it is a good ingredient to add to foods with a lot of seasoning or garlic. Parsley leaves can also be chewed to freshen the breath and cleanse the palate. The leaves have a nice bright green color, which makes them especially pretty in flower arrangements and wreaths.

Recommended:
Curly leaf parsley *(Petroselinum crispum)*
Italian flat-leaf parsley *(P. crispum* var *neapolitanum)*

Rose

Rosa spp.

PERENNIAL

Description: The rose is a beloved flower which is as much adored today as it was hundreds of years ago. But is it an herb? You bet! It is used in cooking, crafting, and potpourri making. It also has numerous medicinal and cosmetic uses which date back thousands of years. It definitely deserves a place in the herb garden.

There are numerous mythological stories associated with roses, as well as many romantic associations. Roses have inspired art, literature, and folklore for thousands of years. The ancient Romans grew tons of roses and the ancient Greeks proclaimed the rose to be "the Queen of all flowers." Even Cleopatra is believed to have had an affinity for this flower. She had the palace floors covered, knee deep, with rose petals when she summoned Mark Anthony.

There are many different species of roses to choose from. Almost all have thorned stems, dark green leaves, and single or double petaled flowers. The roses mentioned in old herbals and stillroom recipes are "old roses" or antique roses, which means they were grown prior to 1867 when hybrids hit the market. To be absolutely authentic, you would want antique roses in your herb garden. But if you already have hybrid teas, you can still use their flowers in recipes. For cooking and crafting, you will generally want to choose the flowers which have the most fragrant petals. Be sure to taste the petals first and choose the ones with the best flavor.

Many old herbals mention the apothecary's rose *(Rosa gallica officinalis)* or the damask rose *(R. damascena).* The petals of these roses were not only used in perfumes, but were also used medicinally. A rose syrup was made with honey for sore throats and a rose vinegar was applied to the forehead to reduce fever.

All roses need full sun and well-draining soil. They are generally heavy feeders and require a lot of water. They are susceptible to blackspot, rust, mildew, and aphids. Many people complain that roses are too much work. But in general, antique roses are more disease-resistant and require less care than the modern hybrid tea roses. If you choose to grow antiques, you will find that they do not take too much care and are well worth the effort. (*See* the "Source Guide" for mail-order sources of antique roses.)

Uses: Rose hips (the seed heads that form after flowering) are packed full of vitamin C. They are used to make tea, jelly, conserves, and wine. The flower petals are used to make syrups and gargles for sore throats. They are very astringent and cleansing, which is why they have a long history as cosmetic ingredients. The petals and essential oils of roses are used in sweet baths, bath oils, perfumes, and soaps. Pure rose essential oil is very expensive because it can take up to 60,000 roses to produce just one ounce of essential oil!

In the kitchen, rose petals can be added to salad, sandwiches, butter, jelly, desserts, and pastries. The petals are sometimes candied and used as a garnish.

Rose flowers and hips are traditionally used fresh in flower arrangements and posies. When dried, they can be used in a number of craft projects including potpourri.

Recommended:
Apothecary's rose *(Rosa gallica officinalis)*
Damask rose *(R. damascena)*
Cabbage or Provence rose *(R. centifolia)*

Rosemary
Rosmarinus officinalis

TENDER PERENNIAL

© Copyright Wheeler Arts

*"... I let it run all over my garden walls, not onlie
because bees love it, but because 'tis the herb sacred to
remembrance and therefore to friendship."*

—SIR THOMAS MORE, UTOPIA

Description: Ancient Greeks believed that rosemary improved memory. They wore wreaths of the herb on their head while studying. In the Middle Ages, sprigs of rosemary were placed under pillows to ward off evil spirits and prevent nightmares. Rosemary has long been considered the symbol for remembrance and love. Brides wore sprigs in their hair and had rosemary in their bouquets. Even today, rosemary is sometimes used in flower arrangements and bridal decorations.

Rosemary is an evergreen herb with aromatic, pine needle-shaped leaves and whorls of blue flowers. There are also white and pink forms. The different cultivars of rosemary can be divided into two groups: upright and prostrate (creeping). Both prefer full sun but will tolerate some shade. The upright rosemaries can grow between 2 and 6 feet tall. They make excellent hedges or shrubs in the garden. The prostrate rosemaries usually stay low to the ground and are perfect for trailing over walls and window boxes. Both types can be grown in pots and shaped into topiaries or bonsai.

Rosemary is best propagated by cuttings or layering. It is a tender perennial, which means that in very cold climates, it must be potted up and brought indoors. Here in Southern California, we are blessed with the perfect climate for rosemary. It grows outdoors all year round and reaches great heights with very little care. In fact, we periodically must cut it back, which allows us to use the thick, fragrant branches as skewers for grilling.

Uses: Fresh and dried rosemary can be added to all meat dishes. It is especially good in beef, game, and lamb recipes. It is also a nice seasoning for breads, vegetables, butters, cheese, soups, and salad dressings. Surprisingly rosemary can also be added to sweet recipes as well. Try it in pastries, cookies, and sorbets.

Rosemary is said to be astringent, antibacterial, and antifungal. Cosmetic uses for rosemary include hair rinses, dandruff shampoo, soap, and herbal baths. In crafting, rosemary is a common ingredient in potpourri and flower decorations.

Recommended:
Creeping rosemary (*Rosmarinus officinalis* 'Prostratus')
Tuscan blue rosemary (*R. officinalis* 'Tuscan Blue')
Pine scented rosemary (*R. officinalis* 'Pine Scented')
White blooming rosemary (*R. officinalis* 'Alba')
Pink blooming rosemary (*R. officinalis* 'Majorica Pink')
Golden rain rosemary (*R. officinalis* 'Joyce DeBaggio')

Sage
Salvia officinalis

PERENNIAL

Description: The genus *Salvia* has literally hundreds of species to choose from. However, no herb garden would be complete without common sage *(Salvia officinalis)*, aka garden sage, with its velvety grayish-green leaves. Keep in mind, though, that there are many other varieties of *S. officinalis* worthy of a place in your herb garden. (*See* the "Recommended" list below.) There are also some ornamental *Salvia* species that are quite beautiful, such as Mexican sage *(S. leucantha)*. It has spikes of fuzzy lavender flowers that are beautiful in flower bouquets and hold their color when dried.

Most sage plants have colorful, long-throated flowers which are very attractive to hummingbirds. Although most are extremely easy to grow, there are a few, such as pineapple sage *(S. elegans)*, that are tender and will not survive harsh winters without being brought indoors. The rest will grow in full sun and can survive with just a heavy mulching for the winter. Most varieties grow to approximately 2–3 feet tall. Sage plants can be propagated by seeds, cuttings, or layering.

Uses: Sage is traditionally combined with thyme, rosemary, and marjoram in the kitchen. It can be used with poultry, pork, beef, venison, and game birds. It also works well in sausage, stuffing, soup, and bread. The flowers of the culinary varieties are edible and can be used in salad or as a garnish.

Sage's astringent and conditioning properties make it invaluable in facial steams, hair rinses, and mouthwashes. It has been used in perfume and soap as well. Its foliage adds fullness to flower arrangements, and the variegated varieties are perfect for handheld posies.

Recommended:
Common sage *(Salvia officinalis):* Culinary
Golden sage *(S. officinalis* 'Aurea'): Culinary
Tricolor sage *(S. officinalis* 'Tricolor'): Culinary
Pineapple sage *(S. elegans):* Culinary
Mexican sage *(S. leucantha):* Ornamental

Santolina
Santolina chamaecyparissus

PERENNIAL

Description: Grey-leaf santolina is a woody shrub with silvery-white leaves that grows to about 2 feet. Although it is sometimes called lavender cotton, it is not a true lavender and is actually a member of the daisy family. It produces mustard yellow, button-shaped flowers in midsummer. The foliage is extremely aromatic and some find it offensive. It has a musky, medicinal scent, which makes it useful as a moth-repelling herb.

During the Elizabethan Era, santolina became a popular knot garden herb. It is extremely easy to shape into hedges and curves. When combined with other santolina species, such as green-leaf santolina *(Santolina virens),* it can create many formal knot garden patterns.

The seeds of santolina are slow to germinate. It is probably best propagated by cuttings or layering. It prefers full sun and does not tolerate humidity very well. It is evergreen in temperate climates, but in cold areas, it will die back and should be mulched heavily to survive any snowy winters.

Uses: With its moth-repelling qualities, santolina sprigs can be placed among linens, woolens, and books. Dried santolina can be made into moth-repellant potpourris and sachets. The leaves hold their color well when dried and make excellent wreaths that are seldom bothered by bugs. The flowers can be dried for potpourri and other crafts. Although the foliage is excellent in flower arrangements, it should not be used in centerpiece arrangements. The strong fragrance may not be appreciated at the dinner table.

Recommended:
Grey santolina or lavender cotton *(Santolina chamaecyparissus)*
Green santolina *(S. virens)*

Savory
Satureja spp.
ANNUAL AND PERENNIAL

Description: There are about 30 species in the genus *Satureja*, but two are commonly grown as savory in American gardens. Summer savory *(Satureja hortenis)* is an annual, and winter savory *(S. montana)* is a perennial. Colonists brought both savories to America as medicinal herbs. They were used to relieve indigestion and soothe sore throats.

Summer savory grows 12–18 inches tall and has long narrow leaves with a delicate, peppery flavor. The flowers are a pinkish-white and are also edible. Winter savory is shorter (about 6–15 inches tall) with a spreading growth habit, which makes it valuable as a border and knot garden plant. It looks and tastes similar to summer savory but has thicker leaves and a stronger flavor. It is hardy to about 10 degrees.

Both savories grow in full sun and are much loved by bees. Summer savory can be propagated by seeds, layering, or cuttings. Winter savory is best propagated by cuttings or division.

Uses: Although both savories can be used in culinary dishes, most cooks prefer the more delicate flavor of summer savory. However, winter savory can be used just as well if young leaves are taken from the tips of the branches.

Savory can be used to season all meat dishes, especially beef and game meats. It is also delicious with beans, eggs, herb butters, and fish.

The leaves of the savory plant can be crushed and rubbed on bee stings to relieve the pain and the itch. Savory foliage is also very attractive in floral bouquets.

Recommended:
Summer savory *(Satureja hortensis)*
Winter savory *(S. montana)*

Scented Geranium
Pelargonium spp.
TENDER PERENNIAL

Description: Although scented geraniums belong to the same botanical family as true geraniums, they are not geraniums at all. They are pelargoniums. They look similar to true geraniums but have aromatic, strongly scented foliage. You can find varieties with sweet fragrances such as rose, lemon, apple, nutmeg, coconut, peppermint, or chocolate! There are records of over 200 different scented geraniums, hybridized from about 75 different varieties. You should definitely grow more than one of these very versatile plants.

Most scented geraniums grow in full sun and are hardy only to about 35 degrees. If you live in a colder area, you will have to dig them up and bring them inside for the winter. What a treat that will be! Scented geraniums do very well in pots and don't mind being grown indoors provided they have a little fertilizer and plenty of light.

Scented geraniums became popular in Europe as houseplants in the 1600s. Their sweetly scented leaves were used for potpourri and tea. They were brought to America with the Colonists and were very popular here as well. Thomas Jefferson grew scented geraniums at the White House.

In the 1800s scented geraniums reached the peak of their popularity when the French began using their essential oil in perfumery. The rose-scented geranium became a cheaper alternative to the extremely expensive attar of rose. During the Victorian Era, scented geraniums were grown in low pots around the parlors so that ladies' dresses would brush them as they passed by, filling the room with fragrance. The Victorians also used them in pastries, desserts, and jellies, as well as floral bouquets.

The flowers of the scented geranium are not spectacular, but these plants are mostly grown for their fragrant foliage. The pretty leaves are well veined and have deep lopes. They range in size from 1/2 inch to several inches, depending upon the variety. They fill the air with scent whenever they are even casually brushed. Scented geraniums should be propagated by cuttings or layering.

Uses: In the kitchen, scented geranium leaves will add subtle flavor to any sweet recipe. They can be used in all kinds of cookies, cakes, desserts, and pastries. Adding the leaves of rose or lemon scented geranium to apple jelly creates a delicious treat.

Known for being slightly astringent, the leaves can be used in cosmetics and facial steams. The leaves can also be dried for potpourri recipes. They hold their fragrance quite well over long periods of time. The essential oil from scented geraniums is used in potpourri making, perfumery, and aromatherapy.

Recommended:
Rose scented *(Pelargonium graveolens)*
Round leaf rose scented *(P. capitatum)*
Variegated rose scented (*P. graveolens* 'Lady Plymouth')
Lemon scented *(P. crispum)*
Lime scented *(P. nervosum)*
Apple scented *(P. ordoratissimum)*
Peppermint (*P. graveolens* 'Tomentosa')
Nutmeg *(P. fragrans)*

Sorrel, French
Rumex acetosa

PERENNIAL

Description: French sorrel is also known as broad-leaf sorrel, common sorrel, or garden sorrel. It has been used since ancient times as a medicinal and culinary herb. The Egyptians ate it to calm the stomach after indulging in rich foods. The Greeks made a tea from sorrel to reduce fevers and cool the body. It is rich in vitamin C and was used to prevent scurvy. It has been considered a popular salad herb since the Medieval days, and today the tangy leaves are popular in French cooking.

Sorrel grows in full sun to partial shade with clumps of bright green, oval-shaped leaves. It reaches 2–3 feet and has reddish-green flower stalks. It is best propagated by seed or division. For a healthy plant, you should dig up and divide sorrel every 2–3 years.

There is another sorrel which is sometimes referred to as French sorrel or buckler-leaved sorrel *(Rumex scutatus)*. Although it is not as common here in America as *R. acetosa,* it is preferred by some cooks because it has a less bitter flavor with a more lemony tang.

Uses: For culinary purposes, sorrel leaves should be picked young, before the plant goes into flower. They can be tossed into salads or sautéed with butter for a quick, delicious sauce. Sorrel goes well with egg and fish recipes. The fresh leaves can also be used to make classic French sorrel soup. Surprisingly, sorrel leaf juice can sometimes bleach out minor rust and mold stains in linen!

Recommended:
Common sorrel *(Rumex acetosa)*
Buckler-leaved sorrel *(R. scutatus)*

Tarragon, French
Artemisia dracunculus var. *sativa*

TENDER PERENNIAL

Description: "True" French tarragon *(Artemisia dracunculus* var. *sativa)* has slender, bright green leaves that have a peppery taste with anise overtones. It gets its name from the French word *esdragon* meaning "little dragon." It was so named because it has dragon- or serpent-type shaped roots. Tarragon grows to approximately 2–3 feet tall and cannot be propagated by seed because it very rarely flowers. Take cuttings or root divisions in early spring.

There is another plant which is sometimes erroneously sold as French tarragon. It is actually Russian tarragon *(A. dracunculoides)*, formerly known as *A. redowskii* and it has an inferior flavor. (If you ever see French tarragon seeds for sale, they are probably Russian tarragon.) Although Russian tarragon is pretty in flower arrangements, it has no value as a culinary herb.

Uses: French tarragon is popular in French cooking and is the primary flavoring in Bearnaise and remoulade sauces. It can be added to many savory foods including: eggs, chicken, fish, and salad dressings. When cooking with tarragon, use a light hand because it can easily dominate other flavors or overpower a dish. Only add it at the end of cooking times or it will taste bitter.

Tarragon is said to stimulate the digestive system. The leaves used to be chewed to numb the taste buds before taking medicine.

Recommended:
French tarragon *(Artemisia dracunculus* var. *sativa)*

Thyme
Thymus vulgaris

PERENNIAL

Description: There are hundreds of different species within the genus *Thymus.* Most can be classified as either upright (10–12 inches) or creeping (2–6 inches), and many are worthy of a space in your garden. The upright varieties are generally the best for culinary use, but the creeping thymes make excellent plants for rock gardens and pathways, releasing their fragrance when stepped upon. They all can be grown in hanging baskets, in window boxes, and along borders.

Indigenous to Mediterranean countries, common thyme *(Thymus vulgaris)* is one of the most popular in American gardens. It is a low-growing, evergreen herb with tiny, aromatic leaves and blossoms. Most thyme plants need full sun and well-drained soil. Continuous clipping promotes bushy growth. After several years, some plants may need to be replaced if they become too woody.

You can grow thyme from seed, but cultivars must be propagated asexually by cuttings, layering, or dividing.

Uses: It has been said, "When in doubt in the kitchen, use thyme." Thyme is extremely versatile as a culinary herb and can be used in just about any savory recipe. Try using it fresh or dried to season beef, fish, poultry, egg, and vegetable dishes. It makes a delicious herb butter and can be added to all kinds of sauces and marinades.

Thyme has many antiseptic qualities. The main oil, thymol, is a powerful antiseptic and explains why thyme has been a successful ingredient in lotions, salves, and mouthwashes.

Thyme is an excellent herb for flower arranging and wreath making because it can withstand long periods of time out of water without wilting. The delicate leaves can also be pressed to create all kinds of decorative crafts.

Recommended:
Common thyme *(Thymus vulgaris)*: Upright
Lemon thyme *(T. x citriodorus)*: Upright
Silver thyme *(T. x citriodorus* 'Argenteus'): Upright
Caraway scented thyme *(T. herba-barona)*: Creeping
Woolly thyme *(T. pseudolanuginosus)*: Creeping

Woodruff, Sweet
Galium odoratum

PERENNIAL

Description: The uses for this woodland plant date back to at least the 1300s, when it was used to scent linens, stuff mattresses, and freshen rooms as a strewing herb. In the medieval days, churches were decorated with sweet woodruff bundles. During the Elizabethan Era, it was extremely popular in wreaths, garlands, and sachets. It is traditionally used in the German celebration of May Day to create Maibowle, or May Wine. (May Wine is made by steeping sweet woodruff in a sweet white wine.)

Sweet woodruff is one of the few herbs which actually prefer shaded areas. It can be grown as an edging plant in a shady section of the herb garden or as a ground cover under trees or shrubs. It does well in pots and looks quite lovely in a hanging basket. It has a spreading habit and only reaches about 6–12 inches tall. Whorls of bright green, pointed leaves form like spokes of a wheel around the stem. The tiny, star-shaped white flowers appear in late spring or early summer. Sweet woodruff can be propagated by seed or root division. It will survive cold winters with just a heavy mulching.

Both the leaves and flowers of sweet woodruff are fragrant. But you will notice that the scent is very subdued while fresh. However, once dried, sweet woodruff smells like a combination of newly mowed hay and vanilla. (You will sometimes see woodruff listed in catalogs by its old name: *Asperula odorata.*)

Uses: The fresh flowers of sweet woodruff can be used in salad or as a garnish in cold drinks. The leaves can be used fresh to flavor May Wine.

Sweet woodruff is best grown for its fragrance and beauty. Dry the leaves and use them in potpourri and other fragrant crafts.

Recommended:
Sweet woodruff *(Galium odoratum)*

Yarrow
Achillea millefolium
PERENNIAL

© Copyright Theresa Loe

Description: Some of the common names for yarrow include soldier's woundwort, carpenter's weed, and nosebleed. The name "soldier's woundwort" comes from its extensive use in treating wounds of all kinds. For centuries, it was a popular wound dressing and was used in this way up to the American Civil War. Native Americans used it to treat many ailments including bruises and sores.

There are many superstitions associated with this herb. One involves young girls placing a flannel sachet of yarrow under their pillows at night, so that they would dream of their future husbands. (Heck, it's worth a try.)

Yarrow is a great way to add color to the herb garden. The blossoms of common yarrow appear as tall, showy clusters of tiny white flowers, with a hint of pink. But you can find varieties with many other striking colors. Some seed companies sell seed mixtures, including pastel varieties which are quite lovely. The leaves of yarrow are long, narrow, and feathery.

Yarrow grows in full sun, to a height of 2–3 feet when flowering. It is a tough and adaptable plant and can become invasive. It can be propagated by seed or division. The seed should only be lightly covered with soil, as it needs some light for germination. As yarrow begins to creep into other areas, you will need to dig up sections and divide them to keep it under control.

Uses: Yarrow flowers work very well in fresh and dried flower arrangements. They hold their color extremely well when dried and can be added to potpourri and other dried craft projects.

Yarrow leaves are astringent and cleansing. They can be used in skin lotions and other cosmetics.

Recommended:
Flaming pink yarrow (*Achillea millefolium* 'Rubra')
Golden yarrow (*A.* x 'Coronation Gold')

Chapter 2

⚬⚬⚬

Getting Started

Happy is the herb gardener through all the seasons and the years. That person enjoys a life enriched with rare fragrances at dawn and dusk and in the heat of noon.

—ADELMA GRENIER SIMMONS

PLANNING AN HERB GARDEN

We all know that a sprawling herb garden with winding paths and hundreds of plants would look spectacular in anyone's backyard, but it would also take a tremendous amount of time (or help) to maintain and use the herbs. If you don't have this kind of time or space, don't despair. Herb gardens come in all shapes and sizes and can be created almost anywhere! Herbs can be added to an existing landscape, planted in a small section of the yard, or even grown in containers on an apartment balcony or windowsill. No matter where you grow your herbs, you simply have to work within your boundaries and choose the herbs which give you the most pleasure.

There are unlimited ways to use herbs in the garden! Creeping rosemary can be placed on the edge of a small raised flowerbed, and in no time at all, it will be gracefully spilling over the edge. Corsican mint, chamomile, and creeping thyme can be planted between stepping stones to create a fragrant, living carpet. Sweet woodruff can be tucked beneath shrubs and shady corners of the yard. Santolina, upright rosemary, and lavender can be used to create fragrant hedges along existing perennial borders.

If you do want to design and plant a large or more complex herb garden, it can be a very rewarding experience as well. If you have the time to maintain them, knot gardens and formally structured herb gardens can be quite dramatic and impressive. If you start out small, you shouldn't have too much trouble with maintenance. You can always add on to the garden later. Just remember, no matter how many herbs you wish to grow, or how much space you have to grow them in, you'll find herb gardening well worth the effort.

No matter what size your finished garden will be, the best place to begin gathering garden ideas is from magazines and garden design books. Collect pictures, ideas, and clippings of what you like or think is appropriate for your garden space. After you have collected some ideas and you want to start formulating your garden design, you should ask yourself the following questions:

1. What do I expect from my garden? If you are interested in growing and using only a few specialized herbs, then you can probably find space for them in your existing landscape. They can be tucked into borders with very little effort. However, if you want to make an architectural impact with your garden, you will need to do some serious planning before you break ground. Think about what your expectations are and plan accordingly.

2. What type of herbs do you want to grow? This may have an influence on the type of design you choose, or you may discover that you want to plant a garden with a particular theme. (*See* "Theme Gardens," below.)

3. How much time do you want to spend gardening? The size and style of a garden directly influence the amount of time involved in maintaining it. For example, a large knot garden must be constantly pruned to keep its formal structure, but a small cottage garden can be neglected for small amounts of time and still look quaint. Before you decide on a design, think about how much time is involved in its upkeep and how much time you have available.

4. Where is the best location for your herb garden? Ideally, you will want a sunny, well-draining location, but do not be discouraged if you have less than ideal conditions. You can work within your limitations with some careful planning. If you do not have full sun, choose herbs which can tolerate partial sun and shade. If you do not have space, you may have to grow smaller herbs such as thyme, basil, and chives. Or you can plant in containers and hanging baskets. As you plan your garden, evaluate the potential site and choose the herbs which fit your conditions.

5. How much space do the plants need? All herbs have different growth habits, and these should be given consideration when laying out the garden plan. Some herbs, such as fennel, need a lot of space to grow, while others, such as thyme, take up very little space. As you choose your herbs for planting, be sure to look up how tall and wide they grow and give them ample space when you do your actual planting. Also, take note of invasive herbs such as mint. You must be careful where you place invasive herbs or they will take over a garden! They should be planted within sunken barriers, in planters, or in pots.

6. How should the garden be laid out? No matter how large or how small your herb garden is going to be, it is smart to draw it out on paper first, to save yourself digging time later. It is much easier to erase than to move an established plant! The general rule of thumb for borders and cottage-style gardens is to place taller herbs toward the back and shorter herbs toward the front. Be sure to include pathways or stepping stones in your design so that you have access to all the herbs for harvesting.

Theme Gardens

If you find yourself drawn to a particular group of herbs with similar uses or colors, you may want to create a theme garden. It can be a fun way to organize the herbs you are planting. For example, if you enjoy fragrant herbs, you may want to create a "pot-pourri garden." If you like cooking with herbs, you might try planting a "culinary garden" or a "tea garden." If you are the whimsical type, a "fairy garden" or a "hummingbird garden" might be more your style. Look over the list below for theme garden ideas.

Beekeepers Garden: Bees are essential to the pollination of many plants and trees in the garden. Since they are attracted to the garden by color (see note) and scent, there are many aromatic herbs they can't resist. If you keep bees or have fruit trees, you may want to include the following bee-loving herbs in your garden: basil, borage, chamomile, dill, fennel, hyssop, lavender, lemon balm, marjoram, oregano, rosemary, sage, savory, and thyme.

Note: Bees are not attracted by the color red. This is because their eyes cannot perceive the long wave lengths in the red end of the spectrum. Many red flowers are pollinated by birds (such as hummingbirds) rather than bees.

Butterfly Garden: Butterflies add beauty and grace to the garden. They are attracted to the garden by color (*see* "Nectar Guides") and scent. (The female butterfly can sometimes smell a plant from up to a half-mile away.) They love many of the same herbs that bees enjoy (*see* list above). If you plant a butterfly garden, however, be prepared to give up some of the foliage to caterpillars.

NECTAR GUIDES

Butterflies and bees see a broader spectrum of light waves then we do, and some plants have developed a way to use this characteristic to their advantage. They attract these pollinating insects to their flowers by emitting what are called "nectar guides." These guides are bands of color (some of which are ultraviolet) that help the insect locate the plant. It is like a flashing neon sign to the butterfly!

Culinary Garden: A culinary or kitchen garden should be planted near the kitchen door so that a cook doesn't have to travel far to gather the fresh herbs. Plant basil, bay, borage, burnet, cilantro, chives, dill, hyssop, lavender, marjoram, mint, nasturtium, oregano, parsley, rose, rosemary, sage, savory, sorrel, tarragon, and thyme.

Fairy Garden: Children love to plant fairy gardens and set out little fairy treats at night. It is a great way to get them involved in horticulture. In case you don't already know, most garden fairies love to play among tiny leaved plants and colorful flowers (but they are very elusive). They are especially partial to Corsican mint, calendula, chamomile, dwarf sage, silver thyme, golden lemon thyme, and rosemary. Be sure to include flowers such as nasturtiums, pansies, primroses, and johnny-jump-ups. They also enjoy all kinds of ferns, moss, and lichens.

Fragrance Garden: Almost all herbs are fragrant, but some are more potent than others. This makes them appropriate for all kinds of crafts, cosmetics, and potpourri. A few of the most aromatic herbs are basil, chamomile, lavender, lemon balm, lemon verbena, mint, rose, rosemary, sage, scented geraniums, and sweet woodruff.

Hummingbird Garden: Hummingbirds absolutely love salvia (sage) plants, so plant as many as you can for these charming little creatures. They are also attracted to brightly colored flowers (especially red) so a mixture of flowers and herbs make a wonderful hummingbird haven. Try growing pineapple sage, Mexican sage, common sage, lamb's ears, mint, scented geraniums, and rosemary. You might also want to include some flowers such as delphinium, lily, red morning glory, or honeysuckle.

Shakespearean Garden: William Shakespeare wrote lovingly of many herbs and flowers. This type of garden is a fun way to celebrate his work. Decorate the garden with painted signs quoting herbal lines from Shakespeare such as, "Here's flowers for you; Hot lavender, mints, savory, marjoram; The marigold that goes to bed wi' the sun; And with him rises weeping . . ." (*The Winter's Tale,* Act IV, Scene III). The following herbs are mentioned in Shakespeare's writings: bay, burnet, calendula, chamomile, hyssop, lavender, lemon balm, marjoram, mint, parsley, rose, rosemary, savory, thyme.

Silver Garden/Moon Garden: A garden of silver-colored foliage can look quite magnificent, especially at night. Try combining the following herbs with white blooming flowers for a moon garden:

clary sage, common sage, grey santolina, lamb's ears, lavender, silver thyme, wormwood, and silver king artemisia.

Tea Garden: Many herbs can be used to create soothing and delicious teas. A tea garden should include chamomile, fennel, hyssop, lavender, lemon balm, mint, rose, rosemary, and scented geranium.

GROWING IN CONTAINERS

If you lack the room for a formal herb garden, container growing may be the solution for you. Herbs do very well in pots and can be moved around a balcony or patio to create a multitude of arrangements. Although they are perfect for apartment dwellers and small space gardeners, anyone can plant and enjoy container grown herbs. Even if you already have an herb garden, you may, at some time, want to plant herbs in pots, hanging baskets, or window boxes. It may be that your herb garden is planted too far from the kitchen and you need a few pots of culinary herbs sitting outside the backdoor. Or you may want to grow an invasive herb, like mint, and need to keep it contained and under control. No matter what the reason, potted herbs are fairly easy to maintain. Watering and occasional feeding will be your biggest chores.

POTTING

A container for herb growing should have drainage holes so that the plants do not become water-logged. (Nondraining containers should be used only if you are willing to monitor them more closely.) You may want to try clay pots, whiskey barrels, strawberry pots, or even unusual containers like wooden boxes or troughs. Choose a container which will accommodate a mature version of the herb you wish to plant. You want the roots to have plenty of room so that the plant will be happy and productive.

The soil used in the containers is important. You generally do not want to use regular soil out of the garden because its chemical and physical makeup is uncertain. It can become hard-packed and it may contain pests and disease spores. Your best bet is to purchase a commercial potting soil. If you feel that the commercial soil is too heavy or poorly draining, then you can add a small amount of perlite for aeration and vermiculite for moisture retention. (Small bags of perlite and vermiculite are available at garden centers.) To get the herbs off to a good start, add a small amount of slow-release fertilizer to the soil mixture. When you are ready to fill a container with soil, remember to place a rock or broken shard of pottery over the drainage holes to prevent the soil from falling out the bottom.

HANGING BASKETS

There are many herbs which lend themselves to hanging basket planting. Try planting mint, pennyroyal, creeping rosemary, sweet woodruff, or thyme.

MAINTENANCE

Once your herbs are potted, you will need to water them regularly. In hot areas, this can be a daily chore. In less arid climates, one to three times a week may be sufficient. You will have to determine your requirements and stick to a regular schedule. Watering is the most labor-intensive part of container growing, especially if you have many potted plants.

Frequent watering will quickly leach the nutrients from the potting soil. Since there is only a limited amount of soil in each pot, this is the one time that a frequent feeding routine should be maintained. A general, all-purpose plant food is fine. This can be a slow-release granule that is sprinkled into each pot, a foliar spray, or a liquid plant food.

Although I have a formal herb garden now, for years I grew my herbs strictly in pots. While renting a very small house a few years back, I grew more than 125 herbs in pots because I had no garden space. Through the years, I found that a monthly treatment

of fish emulsion or manure tea and an occasional feeding with an all-purpose liquid food kept the plants extremely lush and green. (When using a commercial plant food, it is usually best to dilute the mixture to half-strength. Too much nitrogen will result in too much foliage and not enough flavor.) For sources of organic fertilizers such as liquid sea kelp, check the "Source Guide" in the back of this book.

MANURE TEA

You can make your own fertilizer called manure tea. Place three cups of steer or chicken manure in some cheesecloth or a burlap bag and tie closed. (Manure is available at most nurseries and garden supply centers.) Place this bag in a 5-gallon bucket of water and steep for two days (The longer it steeps, the stronger it gets.) Then, remove the "tea bag." Add about 1 cup of this "tea" to 1 gallon of water and use this mixture to give your potted plants a light feeding about once a month.

HARVESTING AND DRYING HERBS

Herbs are so versatile that you will find yourself constantly picking sprigs for a variety of uses. This mild harvesting of your herbs will encourage plant growth and allow you to control the shape and size of the plant. But occasionally, you might want to harvest large quantities of your herb plants as they reach their peak. What can't be used fresh can be dried and stored in airtight containers for later use. During the winter months, when your herb choices and quantities are limited, your dried herbs will come in handy. Nothing should go to waste. The leaves, flowers, and seeds can be used in cooking or crafting. (The seeds can also be saved to plant next year.) The leftover herb stems can be used as fireplace starters (Chapter 9) or grilling herbs (Chapter 4). If your dried herbs become too old for culinary purposes, they can be used as grilling herbs also.

People usually associate harvesting with autumn. But herbs can be harvested throughout the growing season. In fact, for the best flavor and fragrance, an herb should be harvested just before it flowers, when its aromatic oils are at their peak. If you are harvesting for flowers only, harvest the plants just as the flowers begin to open. Seeds should be harvested when they are just ripened and about to drop to the ground.

Always harvest on a dry day, preferably in the morning before the heat of the sun has hit the foliage. Gather the harvested herbs into small bundles and tie using rubber bands. As the herb stems dry, they tend to shrink and the rubber band will shrink with them, thereby preventing the bundles from falling apart. Hang the herb bundles in a warm, dry area, out of direct sunlight. If it is humid, you may want to use a fan to increase circulation. If you are collecting the herbs for seeds, place the herb bundles inside paper bags with the stems sticking out and hang as usual. The bag will allow air to circulate but will also collect falling seeds as the herbs dry.

OVEN DRYING

Herbs can be successfully dried in the oven too. Place the herb leaves onto cookie sheets. Place them in an oven with the pilot light on or turn the oven on to its lowest setting. Leave the door ajar to let moisture escape. Be sure to watch the herbs closely. You don't want them to burn!

Depending upon the density of the leaves and the time of the year, your herbs should dry between seven and ten days. When completely dry, the leaves will be crisp and brittle. At this point, strip the leaves from the branches and place them in clean glass jars. Be sure to label and date the containers. Dried herbs are best used within one year for maximum flavor and fragrance. The jars should be stored out of direct sunlight such as in a dark cupboard.

Check the newly sealed jars after a few days. If moisture is visible, the herbs were not completely dry. They must be removed and redried to prevent mold from forming. (For more information on how to store herb flavors for later use, *see* Chapter 4, "Preserving and Using the Garden's Bounty.")

Chapter 3

The Basics

Most herbs are extremely easy to grow because they can tolerate a wide range of conditions and they generally have only three requirements:

1. Sunshine (though some herbs can grow in shade).
2. Some protection from harsh elements such as heavy wind and extreme cold.
3. Well-draining, moderately fertile soil.

SUNSHINE

Sun intensity varies in different regions, but for most areas, herbs need 6–8 hours of light per day to be at their best. This is considered "full sun." A full-sun location will produce lush plants with essential oil production at its peak. However, there are a few "full-sun" herbs which can tolerate partial shade (and some herbs which prefer shade). Just keep in mind that when "full-sun" herbs are grown in less than 6 hours of light per day, they might have a weaker flavor or fragrance and they might get leggy. The herbs which prefer shade, such as Corsican mint and sweet woodruff, do very well in partial shade with little change in growth habits. (Check the plant descriptions in Chapter 1 for the sun preferences of individual herbs.)

PROTECTION FROM THE ELEMENTS

Extremes in wind, temperature, and humidity can be difficult on all plants, and herbs are no exception. Although herbs will tolerate quite a bit before showing signs of stress, some of the following special circumstances can pose problems.

A windy area will tend to dry out the soil and damage plant foliage. If that wind is a cold one, it can do more damage than just extremely low temperatures alone. Windblown herbs will require extra water and staking. Hedges, fences, and walls are excellent solutions to this problem and add to the herb garden design.

If you live in an area with harsh, cold winters, be sure to note the climate considerations in the plant descriptions. Plants listed as "tender perennials" (such as rosemary) need to be brought indoors during cold winter months. Just pot them up and keep them by a very sunny window. (First let them sit outdoors in the pot for one week, to get over the shock of being uprooted.) While indoors, the dry, heated air can pose a problem for your herbs. Be sure to check the soil moisture often and water only if needed. Most other perennial herbs will do well in the winter with a heavy mulching for protection. Of course, annual herbs do not pose a problem because they are replanted each spring.

> **Note:** Herbs such as bay, lemon verbena, pineapple sage, rosemary, and scented geranium do very well in pots. If you live in a Northern climate, you may want to grow these herbs in containers all year round so that a winter move indoors will be more convenient for you and the plants. Although they will not thrive indoors during the winter months, they should survive until spring. Watch closely for pests while indoors.

If high temperatures are your problem, you may want to plant your herbs in an area with afternoon shade to protect against the burning rays of the sun. Be sure not to water your herbs during the heat of the day or the leaves will steam. Early mornings and evenings are the best times to water. A drip system would be a good option for watering because there is less evaporation and the water would only go where needed.

Another problem with high temperatures is that some herbs such as cilantro and parsley will bolt in the heat and go to seed too quickly. To prevent this from happening, try to keep the flowers pinched off as much as possible. Planting these herbs in partial shade may help. Sometimes, certain perennial herbs will succumb to extreme heat. If this happens, you should treat them as annuals and replant them each spring.

If you live in a humid area, you have a difficult problem. Some herbs, especially gray-leaved herbs, are very affected by humidity. They tend to get powdery mildew and do not look very attractive when the temperature and humidity rise. If you want to grow silver-leaved herbs such as lamb's ears, lavender, or grey santolina, you will have to plant them in dry, sunny areas and hope for the best. This is another case where drip watering would be very beneficial. The less moisture you put on the leaves, the better.

Soil

Good soil is the key to any gardener's success. It provides nutrients and moisture to plants as well as giving them structural support. Soil is a combination of rock particles, organic matter, water, air, and microorganisms. It can vary from hard-packed clay to granular sand.

Clay soil tends to saturate with water easily. The soil is so hard packed, it causes the water to puddle up, thereby drowning the plants. Clay soil may have lots of nutrients but they are not readily available to the roots. On the other hand, sandy soil is the exact opposite. It is very drying to the roots because the water moves through too quickly. It usually lacks nutrients because they are washed out of the soil with the water.

The best soil is a combination of clay, sand, and humus called loam. It is light enough to allow air, water, and nutrients to move through the soil without drying out too quickly. For herbs, it is very important that the soil be well draining. With few exceptions, herbs do not like to have their feet wet all the time.

If you are planting a large area, you may want to invest in a soil analysis from your local community extension service or other soil lab. The test is relatively inexpensive and will provide you with a detailed report about what type of soil you have, what minerals are lacking, and what can be added to improve your soil.

MULCHING

No matter what type of soil you have, it will always benefit from the addition of compost and organic matter. Organic matter will loosen hard-packed clay soil and will help sandy soil retain moisture. It will also add natural nutrients to the soil, thereby feeding the plants. One way to add organic matter to your soil is through mulching.

Mulch is multifunctional. It helps to keep the soil cool in the summer and warm in the winter. It reduces weeds and helps retain moisture. As it breaks down, it adds nutrients to the soil and improves the soil for future generations of gardens.

The best mulch is the free kind you gather from your garden or neighborhood, i.e., homemade compost, grass clippings, chopped leaves, shredded brush, shredded bark, straw, or a mixture of any of the above. You can also buy bags of commercial mulches from your local garden center, but it can be expensive for large areas. For best results, place 2–3 inches of mulch over your herb garden twice a year: spring and fall. This is a natural way to slowly feed and improve your garden.

FERTILIZING

Herbs will thrive in only moderately fertile soil. In fact, if you overfertilize, you will have fast-growing foliage which lacks intense flavors and has very few flowers. Your best bet is to work on improving the soil each year, by adding organic matter as a mulch in the fall and spring rather than feeding with a commercial fertilizer. As the organic matter breaks down, it will energize the herbs naturally without overfeeding. If you still want to feed your plants occasionally, use an organic plant food which is diluted to half-strength.

The one time you will definitely want your herbs to be on a regular feeding schedule is when they are grown in containers. Frequent watering of container herbs will wash away the nutrients in the soil. Therefore, it is usually best to feed potted herbs frequently with a weak solution of liquid fertilizer. (*See* "Growing in Containers" in Chapter 2 for more information on feeding potted herbs.)

PROPAGATION

Propagation is a wonderful way to increase the number of plants in your garden, pass on your favorite plants to friends, and save money in the process!

SEEDS

Seed planting is probably the most versatile propagation method because there is such a wide assortment of herb seeds and they are fairly easy to obtain through mail-order or local garden centers. This makes herb plants accessible to almost anyone regardless of where they live. (*See* the "Source Guide" for mail-order companies.) You will find that there are seeds available for most herbs with the exception of some hybrids (which are either sterile or do not reproduce reliably from seed) and some herbs such as French tarragon, which very rarely produces seeds at all. (These types of herbs must be propagated from cuttings.)

Annual seeds are the easiest to grow because they germinate and mature faster than perennials. But with a little patience, many perennials can be sown from seed as well. Herbs can be sown directly into the garden or started indoors. (Borage, basil, chervil, dill, and parsley do not like to be transplanted and are best sown directly outside.)

For indoor planting, you will need clean, well-draining containers to sow your seeds. If you are doing a large number of seeds, you may wish to purchase a seedling flat from a nursery. Fill your containers three-quarters full with a sterile growing medium. This can be a soilless mix you buy at the garden center or it can be a mixture you prepare yourself. (There are probably as many growing medium recipes as there are gardeners, but one of the easiest combinations is equal parts commercial potting mix, peat moss, and perlite.)

Moisten your growing medium well and firm it down with your hands. If you are planting flats, sprinkle your seeds in rows about 2 inches apart. If you are planting individual containers, place a few medium-sized seeds into each pot or lightly sprinkle very small seeds over the surface of each pot. Cover with a thin layer of growing medium to a thickness approximately two to three times the diameter of the seed you are planting. Extremely fine seeds do not need to be covered; just press them down into the medium.

After planting, be sure to label your containers with the plant name and water lightly. Then, cover the containers with either a plastic bag or plastic wrap to hold in moisture until the seeds sprout. Except where noted below and in the plant profiles in Chapter 1, most seeds do not need light to germinate. Be sure to read the seed packet for any specific instructions.

Note: Chamomile, dill, feverfew, lemon balm, and yarrow must have light to germinate. Do not cover these seeds with dark plastic. The larger seeds can be very lightly covered with soil, but smaller seeds should just be pressed into the soil with no covering.

After the first two true leaves of the plant appear, your seedlings can be transplanted to individual pots until they are large enough to go outside. Harden off the seedlings before planting outside by gradually introducing them to the outdoors a few hours each day for several days. After about 1 1/2 weeks, they will be acclimated to the outdoors and will be ready for planting.

CUTTINGS

Most plants have the ability to regenerate themselves from small pieces of the stem called "cuttings." Soft-stemmed herbs are the easiest to propagate in this manner. Cuttings can be taken throughout the growing season, but fresh, new growth is the best candidate for a cutting.

Prepare pots or flats of a sterile growing medium for your cuttings. You can use the seedling mixture described above or you can use 100% perlite as your growing medium. Use a clean knife to cut a 3–5-inch, nonflowering sprig of the herb just below a leaf node (the place where the leaves join the stem). Remove the leaves from the lower half of the cutting. Dip the lower portion of this cutting into a powdered root hormone (available at your local garden center). Use a stick or pencil to make a small hole in your moistened growing medium and carefully place in the sprig and firm the medium around the stem. Water lightly. Create a mini-greenhouse by covering the pots with clear plastic which is held up with sticks above the actual cuttings. (You can also use an inverted glass jar in place of the plastic.) Keep the cuttings moist, out of direct sunlight, and covered until they show signs of growth, which means they have begun to root. Then, remove the clear plastic. Transplant to the garden after they show sufficient growth and the outdoor soil is warm.

DIVISION

Through the years, your herbs might become too big for their original location. Fortunately, some herbs such as chives, lemon grass, marjoram, mint, oregano, sorrel, tarragon, sweet woodruff, and yarrow grow in clumps which can be dug up when they become too large and divided into pieces for replanting. This process is called dividing and it should be done in the early spring or the fall, when the plants are fairly dormant. Although dividing temporarily sends the plants into shock, they will quickly bounce back if you divide gently and plant the divisions immediately.

To divide one of the herb plants listed above, simply dig up the entire clump. If you can't use your hands to divide the clump, use a clean knife or sharp shovel to separate the root ball into two or three smaller clumps. Immediately replant one of the clumps in the original location and plant the other clumps in another area (or pot them up for a friend). Water them well. Mix a weak solution of plant food (fish emulsion or liquid seaweed) and feed the transplanted divisions to encourage establishment.

LAYERING

Layering is the propagation method used to encourage plants to develop roots along their branches. These rooted branch sections can be severed from the mother plant to continue to grow on their own. There are several herbs which can be layered, including lavender, lemon balm, marjoram, mint, rosemary, sage, santolina, savory, scented geranium, southernwood, and thyme. Some herbs root in only a few weeks while others may take several months. But in either case it is a very simple way to propagate.

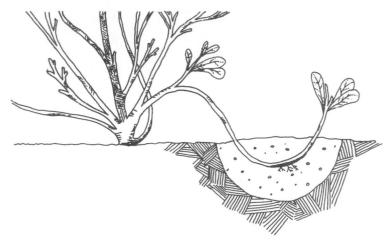

© Copyright Theresa Loe

Layering must be done during the growing season. Early spring is best. First, choose a low branch from the mother plant which can easily bend down to the ground. Hold the branch at about 8 inches from the end and press it down, taking note of where it comes in contact with the soil. At this point on the underside of the branch, wound the area by scratching off the outer layer of the plant stem. Sprinkle the wounded area with rooting hormone (available at the garden center). At the contact point in the soil work in a few handfuls of compost. Gently bend the branch down to the ground and bury it under a few inches of soil, being careful to leave at least 6 inches of branch tip above ground for photosynthesis. Use a rock or a U-shaped piece of wire to secure the branch in place and water well. Watch the layered piece carefully. When new growth begins, you can check under the soil for roots. If roots have formed, sever the plant from its mother but leave it in place for a few more weeks before transplanting.

Herbs in the Kitchen

Even if you have never cooked with herbs before, there is no reason to feel intimidated by these wonderful culinary plants. Just remember that, as with any cooking, herbal flavoring is truly a judgment call, with the cook deciding what suits her taste buds. Just follow the basic guidelines given below, and soon you will find that herbs have introduced you to a whole new world of culinary expression! If you are already an experienced herbal cook, the upcoming recipes should help further inspire your culinary adventures!

As you probably already know, a good cook always tastes the dish throughout the cooking process, not just at the end. This is especially important when using herbs in cooking. You will find that some herbs such as bay, oregano, rosemary, sage, and thyme need long cooking times in order to infuse their flavors into a dish. On the other hand, more fragile herbs, such as basil, cilantro, dill, parsley, salad burnet, and tarragon, must have short cooking times because they lose their flavorful oils rapidly when exposed to heat. For this reason, it is common for these fragile herbs to be used "raw" as a last-minute addition in some recipes.

The amount of chopping you do can also have an effect on the flavoring power of an herb. Whole leaves and coarsely chopped leaves do not fully release their volatile oils. However, when these leaves are finely chopped or minced, their oils are more fully released, thereby intensifying the flavors.

A mortar and pestle or a food processor can maximize this oil release.

When herbs are dried, these flavorful oils slowly lose their potency over time. The longer the herb sits on the pantry shelf, the less flavorful it will become. Therefore, fresh herbs and freshly dried herbs have a superior flavor in recipes. This is why it is important to use up dried herbs within a year if possible.

When cooking, keep in mind that a dried herb is a more concentrated form of a fresh herb. As herb leaves dry, they shrink and you actually have more herb leaves in the dried version than you may realize. When substituting dried herbs for fresh in recipes, only add half as much of the dried version. For example, if a recipe calls for 1 teaspoon fresh sage, use 1/2 teaspoon dried sage as a substitute. (When substituting a fresh herb for a dried, start out using twice as much of the fresh herb. If more is needed, you can add it later.)

As you work with herbs, you will learn that "season to taste" implies much more than just an increase in the salt and pepper. It suggests the addition of any number of aromatic herbs fresh from the garden! Be experimental and enjoy the flavors that these plants have to offer.

Chapter 4

⚜

Preserving and Using
the Garden's Bounty

There is a huge array of methods for preserving the flavors of herbs for later use. Air drying herbs is probably the most common preservation method. (For information on herb drying techniques, *see* "Harvesting and Drying Herbs" in Chapter 2.) Although air drying is the most common and the easiest preservation method, it is important to know that it is not necessarily the best method for all herbs. Delicate herbs such as basil, chives, cilantro, dill, fennel, parsley, and tarragon tend to lose flavor when dried. Although they can be used in the dry state, they actually retain a more potent flavor when stored in a frozen state. They can be frozen quite successfully as "ice cubes" or as concentrated pastes. Although the freezing process causes herbs to lose texture, they will retain their wonderful flavors. Herb flavors can also be preserved by creating herb butters, sugars, syrups, jellies, and vinegars.

FREEZING HERBS

As you can see from the two methods listed below, preserving herbs by freezing is a very simple process. Herbs stored in this way can be used in liquid recipes such as soups, stews, marinades, or sauces.

METHOD 1

1. Wash and pat dry the herb leaves you wish to preserve.
2. These leaves can be chopped and stored directly inside small freezer bags or mixed with water and frozen in ice cube trays.
3. If you choose to make herbal ice cubes, place them inside freezer bags after they are frozen for easy storage.
4. Be sure to label and date the freezer bags because, once frozen, the herbs are indistinguishable.

METHOD 2

1. Gather a large handful of herb sprigs such as basil, tarragon, or dill.
2. Wash the herbs, but do not pat dry.
3. Stuff these sprigs very tightly into a small container with a lid. Stuff as many herbs into the container as possible.
4. Label and freeze.
5. When you want to use the herbs, just remove the whole frozen block and chop off the amount you need. The leaves chop nicely while frozen. Measure and use the herbs as if they were fresh.

HERB PASTE

Herb pastes are similar to pestos except that there are only two ingredients: herb leaves and oil. You'll be surprised at how flavorful and versatile herb pastes can be! They can be used in sauces, marinades, stews, or soups. You can use them to create a quick herb butter or cream cheese dip. You can also use them as a "rub" on beef, chicken, or fish.

Pastes can be frozen as "ice cubes," or they can be stored in small containers. The oil coats the herb leaves and helps to retain the color. It also helps prevent the paste from becoming "rock hard" while frozen. This means that you can scrape a spoon across the top of the frozen paste and remove small amounts for cooking without defrosting the entire container. When cooking with the paste, just add 1/2 teaspoon at a time to get the desired amount of flavor. (Remember, it is concentrated.) With a small stash of pastes in the freezer, you'll have an ample supply of concentrated flavor at your fingertips throughout the year!

> **Note:** You should begin by making a paste from only one herb at a time. Later you can experiment with combinations such as poultry paste: basil, rosemary, and sage; or an Italian paste: oregano, thyme, and marjoram.

1. Place fresh herb leaves into a food processor or blender and process until finely chopped.
2. While the processor or blender is running, slowly add a vegetable oil, one tablespoon at a time. Only add enough oil to coat the herbs and form a paste. You do not want it to be too runny.
3. Remove the paste and either store it in an airtight container or place it into an ice cube tray to freeze before storing in a freezer bag.
4. Be sure to label the containers with the herb name and date. Freeze and use within six months for best flavor.

HERB BUTTERS

Herb butters are a very simple way to add flavor to a meal. Typically they are used on breads and vegetables, but they can also be used to create delicious sauces, marinades, and basting mixtures. If you add a few spoonfuls of herb butter to hot pasta, you have a quick and easy meal.

Butters can be used fresh or they can be frozen in plastic wrap for later use. Be sure to label and date your frozen butters and use within four months for best flavor. Keep in mind that the basic recipe for herb butter can be changed to suit your needs. For example, a basting sauce may need a stronger flavor than a butter to be used on bread and would therefore have more herbs added. Try adding chopped shallots, scallions, dried red peppers, or grated citrus peel to your recipes for a more intense flavor. Be creative with your herb combinations!

Basic Herb Butter Recipe

1 stick softened butter (1/2 cup)
approximately 2 tbsp. chopped fresh herbs (1-3 different kinds)
other flavoring such as spices, citrus peel or garlic

Rosemary-Garlic Butter (for bread and vegetables)

1. Mix 2 tbsp. freshly chopped rosemary into the softened butter.
2. Add 1 clove of minced garlic and mix well.
3. Let mixture sit in the refrigerator for several hours before using.

Dill Butter (for bread and vegetables)

1. Mix 1 tbsp. dill weed, 1 tsp. dill seed, and 2 tsp. freshly chopped parsley into the softened butter.
2. Let the mixture sit in the refrigerator for several hours before using.

Lemon Herb Butter (for steamed green beans, asparagus, fish, or poultry)

1. Mix 1 tbsp. each of freshly chopped lemon thyme and lemon balm into the softened butter.

2. Add 2 tsp. grated lemon zest (the yellow portion of the peel).
3. Store in the refrigerator for several hours before using.

Tarragon Mustard Butter (for sandwiches, chicken, bread and vegetables)

1. Mix 1 tbsp. freshly chopped tarragon and 2 tsp. freshly chopped chive blossoms.
2. Add 1 tbsp. prepared mustard (regular, spicy, or Dijon) into the softened butter.
3. Store in the refrigerator for several hours before using.

HERBAL SPICE BLENDS

Herb blends can be used in place of salt in some recipes and are helpful in spicing up bland, fat-free diets. If you aren't counting calories, try adding herb seasonings to sour cream or cream cheese to create sinfully delicious dips and hors d'oeuvres.

There are numerous benefits from creating flavorful herb blends straight from your garden:

1. You can customize the seasonings to your own personal preferences.
2. You can be assured that the blends you create are completely free of preservatives, additives, and pesticides.
3. The ingredients are freshly dried and therefore have superior flavor and a longer shelf life than commercial blends.
4. The ingredients are free!
5. Herbal blends make inexpensive gifts for family and friends.

The following recipes yield small batches of seasonings so that you can experiment freely without feeling wasteful. However, they can easily be doubled or tripled for storage on your pantry shelf or for gift giving. Just be sure to use them up within one year for best flavor. Once you have tried a few of the following blends, don't be afraid to develop a few of your own!

To make the following herb seasonings, combine all ingredients and store in an airtight jar or container. Use 1 or 2 teaspoons at a time in recipes until you get the desired level of flavor.

Beef Seasoning

This simple blend can be used in any red meat recipe.

1 tbsp. dried rosemary
1 tbsp. dried savory
1 tbsp. dried thyme
1 tbsp. dried parsley
1 tsp. garlic powder
1 tsp. ground black pepper

Poultry Seasoning

Sprinkle some of this seasoning on chicken or turkey. It can also be added to soups and casseroles.

1 tbsp. dried sage
1 tbsp. dried thyme
1 tbsp. dried marjoram
1 tsp. dried tarragon
1/4 tsp. ground white pepper

Seafood Seasoning

This recipe includes dill weed, which is the leafy portion of the dill plant, and dried lemon peel. You can use a commercially prepared dried lemon peel, which is available in the spice section of the supermarket, or you can dry your own. To dry the lemon peel, grate the zest (the yellow portion of the peel) of one lemon. Place it on a cookie sheet, in the oven, on its lowest setting. Watch closely and remove when completely dry (30 minutes–1 hour). Use some of this seasoning during cooking of any fish recipe or combine with butter for a fast seafood sauce.

2 tbsp. dried dill weed
1 tsp. dried dill seed
1 tbsp. dried lemon thyme (or common thyme)
1 tsp. dried lemon balm
1 tsp. dried lemon peel
1 tsp. fennel seeds

Vegetable Seasoning

This unusual blend can be combined with butter as a vegetable sauce, sprinkled over cooked vegetables, or added to the water of steaming vegetables.

2 tbsp. dried mint
1 tsp. dried lemon thyme (or common thyme)
1 tsp. celery seed

Popcorn Seasoning

Sprinkle approximately 1 tbsp. of this flavorful combination over freshly buttered popcorn for a new treat!

2 tbsp. dried oregano
1 tbsp. dried basil
2 tsp. salt (optional)
1 tsp. garlic powder
5 tbsp. Parmesan cheese

Italian Seasoning

Add this blend to spaghetti sauces, bread, lasagne, pasta, or anything requiring a taste of Italy.

2 tbsp. dried oregano
2 tbsp. dried thyme
1 tbsp. dried basil
2 tsp. dried rosemary
1/2 tsp. garlic powder

GRILLING HERBS

Dried herbs will lose much of their flavor after a year of sitting on the spice shelf. But don't throw them away! They can still be used as grilling herbs. Next time you are grilling meat or vegetables, sprinkle some of the dried herbs over the coals and close the lid. The burning herbs will give off a flavorful smoke which will help season the food! You can also accomplish the same thing with fresh herb sprigs. Toss a few bay leaves or sage sprigs over the coals the next time you are grilling beef or chicken!

Herbal Syrup

ℴℯ✠ℯℴ

Herbal syrups are a very simple and "sweet" way to preserve herb flavors for later use. The finished syrups have a multitude of uses. Try them as sweeteners in hot tea or cold fruit drinks. They can be drizzled over cakes, ice cream, pastries, or fresh fruit. You can make syrup with almost any sweet herb such as lemon verbena, lemon balm, mint, rose petals, scented geraniums, or lavender. The herbs will color the liquid slightly, but if more color is desired, add a few drops of food coloring.

INGREDIENTS:

1-1 1/2 cups sugar
1/2 cup water
1 cup hard-packed fresh herbs

1. In a medium-sized sauce pan, combine all ingredients over medium-high heat. Bring to a boil, reduce heat, and simmer 3 minutes.
2. Remove from heat and set aside to cool completely. When cool, strain the mixture and pour into a decorative bottle with a tight-fitting lid.
3. Store in the refrigerator and use within 3 months.

Lemon Herb Syrup: Follow the recipe above using 1 1/2 cups sugar, 1/2 cup water, 1/2 cup lemon balm, 1/2 cup lemon verbena, and the yellow portion of one lemon peel. (You can use a potato peeler to easily remove peel.)

Mint Syrup: Follow the basic recipe using 1 cup sugar, 1/2 cup water, and 1 cup hard-packed spearmint or peppermint.

Rose Petal Syrup: Follow the basic recipe using 1 cup sugar, 1/2 cup water, and 1 1/2 cups fresh red or pink rose petals from fragrant roses. Stir in 1 tbsp. of rosewater after the mixture has cooled completely.

Herbal Sugar

Another "sweet" way to preserve the flavor of herbs is by making infused sugars. When the finished sugars are used in baking, pastry making, candy making, etc., they impart some of their delicate flavors into the baked goods. Herbal sugars can also be used to sweeten tea and fruit drinks. Any of the sweet herbs can be used: lemon verbena, lemon balm, mint, rose petals, scented geraniums, or lavender.

INGREDIENTS:

2 cups sugar
1 cup fresh herbs (choose one of the herbs listed above)

1. In a glass jar, place alternating layers of sugar and herbs, being sure that all the herb leaves are completely covered with sugar. Cover tightly with an airtight lid.
2. Set mixture aside for 2–3 weeks. Strain the sugar through a coarse sieve, removing all the herbs.
3. Store infused sugar in an airtight container and use within six months.

Herbal Jelly

One of the easiest ways to make a flavorful herb jelly is to add herbs to a plain apple jelly. The apple flavor combines well with both sweet and savory herbs, creating a unique condiment. Jellies made with lavender, scented geranium, roses, or lemon verbena can be used on toast, scones, or desserts. Jellies made with mint, basil, rosemary, sage, or thyme are excellent condiments when served with various meat dishes.

INGREDIENTS:

5 cups sugar
extra herb leaves or sprigs for decoration in jar
4 cups apple juice
1 1/2 cups firmly packed fresh herbs
1 3/4 oz. package powdered pectin
6-7 canning jars with screw top lids—washed and
*   sterilized in hot water*

1. Measure sugar and set aside. Place an extra herb sprig in the bottom of each clean, sterilized canning jar.
2. Combine apple juice and fresh herbs in a large sauce pan over medium heat. Bring to a boil. Let the mixture boil 1

minute, then remove from heat and set aside to cool
completely (about 1 hour).

3. Strain out and discard the herbs.
4. Combine cooled apple juice and powdered pectin in a large
   sauce pan. Bring to a rolling boil (one that cannot be stirred
   down) and boil hard 1 minute.
5. Add the measured sugar and bring the mixture to a rolling
   boil again. Allow mixture to boil hard for 1 minute. Then
   remove from heat and skim off foam if necessary.
6. Ladle jelly into clean, sterilized canning jars. Wipe off the
   tops of the jars and place on the lids and rings. Tighten
   the jar rings until they are just snug; not too tight or too
   loose.
7. Process the finished jelly in a water bath for 10 minutes.
   Remove and let cool. Check the seal on each jar by pressing
   down on the lid. If it pops up and down in the center, it is
   not sealed. All unsealed jars should be stored in the
   refrigerator and eaten within 2 weeks. Sealed jars can be
   stored in the pantry and used within 1 year.

YIELD: SIX 8 OZ. JARS

LIQUID PECTIN

*Liquid pectin may be substituted for powdered in the
above recipe. However, the cooking sequence is a little different. To use liquid pectin, follow the above recipe substituting Steps 4 and 5 as follows:*

4. Combine cooled apple juice and measured sugar in a
   large sauce pan. Bring to a rolling boil (one that cannot be stirred down) and boil hard 1 minute.
5. Add liquid pectin and bring mixture to a rolling boil
   again. Allow mixture to boil hard for 1 minute. Then remove from heat and skim off foam if necessary. Continue with Step 6 above.

Rose Geranium Jelly: Follow the basic jelly recipe using 1 1/2-2 cups fresh rose geranium leaves as the herb. After the jelly is completely cooked, add 2 tbsp. rosewater and stir well. Before ladling the jelly into the jars, place one fresh rose geranium leaf in the bottom of each jar.

Rose Petal Jelly: Follow the basic jelly recipe using 2 cups of fresh red or pink rose petals from very fragrant roses. After the jelly is completely cooked, add 1 tbsp. rosewater and stir well. Don't bother adding a rose petal to each empty jar; they tend to turn brown and look unattractive when the hot jelly is ladled in.

Note: To prepare the rose petals for jelly making, you should rinse them under cool water. Pull the petals off and blot them dry between two tea towels. Rose petals have a very distinctive white or yellow portion at the base of the petal (where the petal joins the flower). Use scissors or your fingers to remove this portion from each petal. (It is bitter and should be removed when cooking with roses.) Then measure and use as directed in the jelly recipe.

HERBAL VINEGARS

Flavored vinegars have become quite popular in recent years and are considered a staple in the gourmet kitchen. They can be used to create delicious salad dressings, marinades, and sauces. You can create your own exotic and unique herbal vinegars with ingredients you grow yourself. They are inexpensive to create and they make wonderful gifts when accompanied by a recipe for their use. Virtually any culinary herb and spice can be used in the creation of flavored vinegars. You are only limited by your own imagination! Use the basic herb vinegar recipe below as a guide for your own creations or use one of the tried-and-true recipes that follow. To use your new creations, a recipe for basic vinaigrette and grilling marinade follow the vinegar section.

VINEGAR BASE

There are several different vinegars on the market that are appropriate for flavoring. The only one I do *not* recommend using is distilled white vinegar. Its flavor is really too harsh and it overpowers the delicate herbal flavors. However, you can use any of the following vinegars with good results.

White wine vinegar: has a light color and very good flavor. It is excellent for delicate herbs or sweet vinegars. It is also good for fruit vinegars.

Red wine vinegar: is ruby red and is best for strong or savory herb vinegars such as rosemary or sage.

Rice vinegar: has a clear color. This vinegar is sweet and is excellent for sweet herb or fruit vinegars.

Cider vinegar: has a caramel color. This vinegar is inexpensive and is fine for almost all herbal vinegars except fruit vinegars. (I prefer rice vinegar or champagne vinegar for sweetly flavored mixtures.)

Champagne vinegar: has a clear color. This is the best of all the vinegars, because it has a very delicate flavor. The down side is that it can be difficult to find in large quantities and it is usually the most expensive of all the vinegars.

GENERAL CONSIDERATIONS WHEN MAKING FLAVORED VINEGARS

1. Never use aluminum pans or utensils for heating or steeping your vinegars. Use enamel or glass containers and wooden spoons. The aluminum can react with the vinegar and produce an off flavor.

2. The longer you steep a vinegar mixture, the stronger the herb flavor will become.
3. Herb vinegar lasts indefinitely on the shelf because the acidity of the vinegar acts as a preservative. However, although it is perfectly safe to use, over time the flavor of herbal vinegar will deteriorate. For best flavor, it should be used within 6 months to a year.
4. You can use a double layer of cheesecloth to strain your vinegars, but the resulting product may not be crystal clear and a sediment might develop at the bottom of the finished bottle. This is not harmful, but is not aesthetically pleasing (especially for gift giving). For a clear vinegar, you should use coffee filters for a third or fourth straining after straining with cheesecloth first. The finished product will look as clear as the commercial brands!
5. Make sure that the fresh herbs you use are completely free from moisture before adding them to the vinegar. Any water on the leaves will result in a cloudy vinegar.
6. There are no hard-and-fast rules when it comes to measuring herbs for these vinegar recipes. The measurements given here are just approximations. You may add more or less of a particular herb as you feel necessary. You will soon discover that you can't go wrong with herb vinegar because they all taste wonderful!
7. Add fresh herb sprigs to the vinegar bottles before pouring in the finished product. It adds a nice decoration and con-

tinues to flavor the vinegar. And remember, herbal flowers such as chive blossoms, borage blossoms, nasturtiums, or other flowering culinary herbs can be used in the steeping process and as decorations in the bottle.

8. Any clean glass bottle can be used to store the finished vinegars. You can use old bottles or you can buy new ones. For mail-order sources of new bottles, *see* the "Source Guide" at the back of the book.

Basic Herb Vinegar Recipe

INGREDIENTS:

4 cups vinegar
1 cup hard-packed fresh herbs
other flavorings such as citrus peel, raspberries, garlic, or
spices

1. Heat the vinegar to very warm but not boiling. Add the herbs and spices. Pour the mixture into a clean glass container. Cover and allow to cool.

2. Let herbs steep for 1–2 weeks at room temperature. Strain the vinegar several times through cheesecloth and/or coffee filters to get a clear liquid.

3. Place a few fresh sprigs of the herb used inside clean glass bottles. Pour the strained vinegar into the bottles. Seal bottles with tight-fitting corks or lids.

4. Label and store your finished vinegars in a cool, dark cupboard. Use within 6 months to 1 year.

YIELD: 4 CUPS

Classic Herb Vinegar Combinations

Rosemary/Garlic Vinegar: 4 cups red wine vinegar, 1 cup fresh rosemary, 5 cloves of garlic (cut in half). Use in salad dressings, beef marinades, and beef sauces.

Lemon Basil Vinegar: 4 cups white wine vinegar, 1 cup fresh lemon basil, the yellow portion of one lemon peel (use a potato peeler to remove peel). Use in salad dressings, poultry, or fish marinades and sauces. (You may substitute another basil for the lemon basil.)

Tarragon Vinegar: 4 cups white wine or champagne vinegar, 1 cup fresh tarragon. Use in poultry or fish marinades and sauces.

More Adventurous Herb Vinegars

Spicy Lemongrass Vinegar: 4 cups rice wine vinegar, 3/4 cup freshly chopped lemon grass, 2 tbsp. black peppercorns, 3 whole red chili peppers, yellow portion of one lemon peel (use a potato peeler to remove peel). After steeping, place a spiral of fresh lemon peel and 1 whole red chili pepper in the finished bottle for decoration. Use in salad dressings, poultry marinades, or Asian cooking.

Fresh Fennel Vinegar: 4 cups white wine or champagne vinegar, 1 cup fresh fennel leaves, 2 tbsp. fennel seed. After steeping, place a fresh sprig of fennel seed (if available) in the finished bottle for decoration. Excellent in salad dressings, vegetable dishes, chicken, pork, and fish marinades.

Salad Burnet Vinegar: 4 cups white wine or champagne vinegar, 1 cup fresh salad burnet, 1/4 cup fresh chives. This vinegar has a distinctive cucumber-like flavor and is delicious in salad dressings, cucumber salads, and vegetable dishes.

Basic Vinaigrette Salad Dressing

Vinaigrette is a great way to utilize a flavorful herbal vinegar and it requires only a few ingredients: oil, vinegar, mustard, salt, and pepper. The basic proportions are 3 parts oil to 1 part vinegar. The amount of mustard used can vary. You can change the flavor tremendously by changing the type of oil or vinegar used. Try olive oil, walnut oil, or vegetable oil in combination with any of the herbal vinegars you create. It is also nice to include some freshly chopped herbs if possible.

INGREDIENTS:

2 tbsp. herbal vinegar
6 tbsp. oil
1 tsp. prepared mustard
1 tsp. freshly chopped herbs
salt and pepper to taste

1. Combine all ingredients in a bowl and whisk until well combined. Pour into a glass jar with a tight-fitting lid. Set aside for at least 10 minutes.
2. Shake dressing again before pouring over fresh salad greens and serving.

Basic Grilling Marinade

This marinade is another way to utilize the vinegars you have made. It can be used on chicken and vegetables when grilling or as a basting sauce on any poultry recipe. Try using different vinegars to get different flavors. It is always nice to include some freshly chopped herbs in the recipe for added flavor. (For example, if you use a dill vinegar, include fresh dill weed in the marinade.)

INGREDIENTS:

1/4 cup herb vinegar
1/2 cup vegetable oil
3 tbsp. honey
1/4 tsp. garlic powder
1 tsp. freshly chopped herbs (optional)

1. Combine all ingredients in a bowl and whisk vigorously. Pour over chicken or vegetables to be marinaded.
2. Cover and refrigerate for 20–30 minutes before grilling.

Chapter 5

Savory Herbs

Hundreds of years ago, when there were no refrigerators or preservatives (other than salt), herbs were used to cover up the off flavors of different meats as they began to spoil. Fortunately, today we don't use herbs for this purpose! Instead, we use them to add extraordinary flavor to otherwise ordinary foods.

Savory herbs are generally used to flavor foods other than

desserts, such as appetizers, main dishes, and side dishes. They usually have a robust flavor and are delicious on their own or in combination with other herbs. Some herbs, such as basil, are useful in both savory and sweet recipes. So you may find a so-called savory herb used in a dessert. As you can see, there are no stringent rules in herbal cooking. Rather, there are just a lot of gray areas which leave the door open to experimentation. That's what makes herbal cooking so fun!

Some of the herbs which can be used in savory recipes are basil, bay, salad burnet, calendula, chives, cilantro, dill, fennel, hyssop, lemon grass, marjoram, nasturtium, oregano, parsley, rosemary, sage, savory, sorrel, tarragon, and thyme. This list is not complete, by any means. But it is a good start for creating delicious meals.

BOUQUET GARNI

One way to add savory flavors to food is with a bouquet garni. (*Bouquet garni* is a French term meaning "bundle of herbs.") It can be made with fresh or dried herbs that are tossed into soups, stocks, sauces, or stews for flavoring. The bouquet garni is always removed before serving. It is a nice way to flavor foods, especially clear soups or stocks, without cluttering up the broth with lots of little herb sprigs and branches.

The classic combination of herbs for a bouquet garni is parsley, thyme, and bay leaf. But you can add or subtract different herbs if you want to. That way, you can create your own bouquet garni combinations for your own specific needs and preferences. However, it is best to use only three or four different herbs at a time.

A fresh bouquet garni can be made by tying together a few sprigs of each herb with a cotton string (like a little posy). For added flavor, you can lay the fresh herb sprigs in a 4-inch piece of celery and tie it with cotton string. You can also wrap up some fresh sprigs of herbs in a blanched leek that is tied securely with cotton string. The leek will add flavor as well as hold the bouquet garni together.

For a dried bouquet garni, combine 1 teaspoon of each herb

inside a cotton tea bag and tie securely. Or tie the dried herbs up in a square of cheesecloth. Either way, the dried bouquet garni will keep the liquid you are cooking flavorful but clear.

Summertime Gazpacho with Fresh Basil and Chives

Basil is a very aromatic herb which has a flavor reminiscent of clove and pepper. This flavor combines well with any tomato dish, especially summertime gazpacho. Gazpacho is a delicious cold soup, which can be served as an appetizer or as a light luncheon meal. Cold soup may be new to some people, but once they taste the refreshing flavor, they will be hooked! Serve it with herbal bread or light sandwiches.

This recipe is a breeze to make if you have a food processor, because it only takes a few minutes and there is no cooking involved. If you don't have a food processor, you can use a blender. Just chop the vegetables into smaller pieces for processing. The finished soup should have some texture and crunch to it. If the soup seems too thick, you can add more tomato juice to thin it.

INGREDIENTS:

4 large, ripe tomatoes (or 5 medium tomatoes)
2 medium green bell peppers, coarsely chopped
1/2 onion, coarsely chopped
2 large cucumbers, peeled and coarsely chopped
1 clove garlic, cut in half
4 tbsp. freshly chopped basil
2 tbsp. freshly chopped chives
1 1/2 cups tomato juice
1 tbsp. lemon juice
1/4 tsp. Tabasco sauce (optional)
salt and pepper to taste
extra chopped chives for garnishing

1. Remove the core on the tomatoes and cut them in half, crosswise. Squeeze out the seeds. (You will lose some juice when you do this.) Then, coarsely chop the seeded tomatoes.
2. Place the tomatoes in the food processor and process until smooth. Pour the tomato puree into a large bowl.
3. Place the bell pepper and onion in the food processor and process until smooth. Pour the resulting puree into the bowl with the tomatoes.
4. Place the cucumber, garlic, basil, chives, and 1/2 cup of the tomato juice in the food processor bowl and process until very smooth and creamy. (Be sure the garlic gets processed well.)
5. Pour this mixture into the bowl holding the tomato and bell pepper puree. Add the remaining tomato juice, lemon juice, and Tabasco. Mix well. (If the soup is too thick, add more tomato juice.) Add salt and pepper to taste. (Use a light hand; the soup's flavor intensifies as it sits in the refrigerator.)
6. Let the soup sit in the refrigerator at least five hours to overnight. Then, taste it to be sure the seasoning is correct. Adjust seasonings if necessary. Serve chilled, with chopped chives sprinkled over the top.

YIELD: APPROXIMATELY 2 QUARTS

Stuffed Nasturtiums

These little gems are fun to make and a delight to eat. They can be served as appetizers or as a festive edible garnish on a luncheon plate. The flowers themselves have a delicate, peppery taste.

INGREDIENTS:

1 eight-ounce package cream cheese, softened
1 tbsp. prepared mustard
1 tbsp. finely minced red onion
2 tsp. freshly chopped parsley
2-3-dozen nasturtium flowers
pastry bag and star tip

1. In a small bowl, combine cream cheese, mustard, red onion, and parsley. Use a fork to combine all the ingredients well. Cover and let the mixture sit in the refrigerator for several hours to overnight.
2. Thoroughly wash the nasturtium flowers and allow them to dry on paper towels.
3. Meanwhile, take the cream cheese mixture out of the refrigerator and let it sit at room temperature for 30 minutes to soften.
4. Spoon the cream cheese mixture into a pastry bag fitted with a large star tip. Pipe the cheese into the individual flowers. Place the stuffed flowers on a plate and store in the refrigerator until ready to serve.

YIELD: **2–3** DOZEN

Herb Bread in Flowerpots

Herb bread just seems to be more delicious when it is served in small clay flowerpots! That's right, flowerpots! This bread is baked and served inside clean, unused flowerpots which have been seasoned with oil to prevent sticking. Once the flowerpots are seasoned, they can be used again and again for bread baking. Just keep them in the kitchen so that no one plants anything in them!

Clay flowerpots are safe for cooking as long as they are clean and American made (some foreign pots have too many impurities). For added safety, you can line the inside of the flowerpots with aluminum foil. (This will also prevent the dough and the herb butter from leaking out of the bottom.)

This recipe calls for using frozen bread dough, which is available from the freezer section of your supermarket. It comes in two forms: loaves or individual rolls. You can use either one for this recipe. If you would rather make your own homemade dough, you can use any standard white bread dough recipe.

This bread is made with fresh rosemary, but you can substitute many different herbs in its place. Try some of the substitution suggestions at the end of the recipe.

INGREDIENTS:

8 small clay flowerpots (clean and unused)
vegetable oil
1 loaf frozen bread dough (or 1 package frozen bread rolls)
1 tbsp. butter, melted
1 stick of butter or margarine
1 tbsp. finely chopped rosemary (see substitutions below)
aluminum foil
Parmesan cheese

1. Wash and dry the flowerpots. Brush the inside of each flowerpot with vegetable oil. Place the pots on a cookie sheet and bake them at 450 degrees for one hour. Remove the flowerpots and set them aside to cool.
2. Meanwhile, remove the frozen dough from the freezer and place it on a greased cookie sheet. Rub the outside of the dough with 1 tbsp. of melted butter to prevent it from drying out. Set the dough in a warm place for several hours or until it has risen to double its original size.
3. Line the flowerpots with aluminum foil. Trim the foil so that it is approximately 1/2 inch below the top of the pot and will not show when the bread is baked inside.
4. After the dough has risen to double the original size, melt 1 stick of butter in a small sauce pan. Add your herbs and stir well. Remove from heat.
5. Break off a piece of dough that is about the size of a golf ball (or take one frozen dough roll). Roll it into a ball and dip it into the herb butter mixture. Coat it well on all sides and place it inside the flowerpot which is lined with foil.
6. Continue until you have 3-4 balls inside each flowerpot. (The flowerpots should be filled about 1/2-2/3 full.) Sprinkle the tops with Parmesan cheese. Set the filled flowerpots in a warm place and let them rise again until they are double in size (approximately 30 minutes).
7. Preheat the oven to 350 degrees. Place the flowerpots on a cookie sheet and bake them for about 12 minutes or until the tops are golden brown.
8. You can serve the bread warm or cold. If you need to reheat the bread before serving, simply cover each flowerpot bread with aluminum foil and place in a 350-degree oven for 10-15 minutes. Keep in mind that if you serve this bread hot, the warm flowerpots will be sitting directly on your table. To prevent them from marking the table, you can set them in clay saucers or on coasters.

Herb Substitutions: You can dramatically change the flavor of your bread by substituting one of the following for the rosemary:

1. 1 tbsp. "Italian Herb Seasoning," from Chapter 4
2. 2 tbsp. freshly chopped chives and 1 clove garlic, minced
3. 1 tbsp. dried dill weed and 1 tsp. dill seed

YIELD: 6–8 FLOWERPOT BREADS

Grilled Focaccia with Savory Herb Toppings

Focaccia is an Italian flat bread. Here the focaccia is grilled on the barbeque. This adds a smoky flavor that you just can't get any other way. This recipe is not as complicated as it sounds. By using frozen bread dough, the preparation time is cut in half. The individual focaccia dough can be prepared up to 24 hours ahead of time and stored in the refrigerator. The toppings can be chopped ahead of time also. Then, when the grill is ready, the bread dough, oil, and toppings are taken out and grilled. Each frozen loaf of bread will yield three focaccias. They will be popular, so to be safe, count on one focaccia per guest.

Once the frozen bread dough has risen, you must be very careful when you handle it. If you overwork it, it will not roll out properly. Instead, it will keep springing back on you. If this happens, set the dough aside for about 15–20 minutes to rest and then try rolling it out again.

You should prepare a few toppings from each topping group listed below. Then, make several different focaccias by using different combinations of those toppings. Have fun with it! You can't go wrong! This bread makes a great appetizer. Grill it right in front of your guests and serve it hot. Or, you can grill it ahead of time and serve it cold on a buffet table. If served cold, use a pizza cutter to slice it.

INGREDIENTS:

2 loaves of frozen bread dough
vegetable oil
cutting board and rolling pin
parchment paper or wax paper
herb and vegetable toppings:

> **Topping Group 1:** *1/4 cup of any of the following herbs (finely chopped): rosemary, sage, marjoram, mint, dill, chives, basil*

> **Topping Group 2:** *1/3 cup of any of the following (finely chopped): scallions, red onion, black olives, mozzarella cheese, Parmesan cheese*

1. Remove the 2 loaves of frozen bread dough from the freezer and place them on greased cookie sheets. Brush each loaf with vegetable oil to prevent it from drying out. Set them in a warm place until they have risen to double their original size (2–3 hours).
2. When the dough is ready, brush your cutting board and rolling pin with vegetable oil to prevent sticking. Use a knife to cut off 1/3 of one loaf. Carefully place this piece of dough on the cutting board without deflating it. Use the rolling pin to roll it out into a free-form circle. (If you have trouble keeping the bread from springing back as you roll it out,

follow the steps detailed in the introduction of this recipe.)

3. Place the rolled-out circle on a piece of parchment paper (or wax paper) and set it on a plate. Place another piece of parchment paper on top of it.

4. Cut another 1/3 piece off the dough loaf and follow the same procedure to roll it out. Place it on the parchment paper stack and place another piece of parchment paper (or wax paper) on top of it. Continue with the remaining bread dough.

5. After all the dough is rolled out, wrap the entire stack of uncooked focaccias with plastic wrap. Place them in the refrigerator until you are ready to grill.

6. Meanwhile prepare a few toppings and place them on a plate in individual piles. Cover with plastic wrap and set them in the refrigerator until you are ready to grill.

Hint: Try adding hickory or mesquite chips to the grill coals just before grilling the bread! This will give the bread a unique hickory flavor that can't be beat! You should be able to find barbeque wood chips wherever you buy charcoal. Soak them in water first so that they will smolder and smoke rather than burn.

To Grill the Bread:

1. When the grill is ready, remove the top piece of parchment paper from the top piece of focaccia dough. Brush the dough with oil to prevent sticking. Sprinkle the dough with your toppings of choice.

2. Carefully place your hand under the piece of parchment paper that the dough is resting on and flip the dough onto the grill (facedown), like a pancake. Immediately remove the back piece of parchment paper and brush that side

with oil while the bottom is grilling. Add your toppings to the exposed side and cover the grill. Cook for 1-2 minutes.
3. Open the grill and use a large spatula to flip the bread. Cover and cook for 1-2 minutes longer.
4. Remove the bread and continue with the next piece of focaccia dough.
5. When all the bread is grilled, serve immediately or let cool and serve cold.

YIELD: 6 FOCACCIAS (3 PER LOAF OF BREAD)

Homemade Herbal Croutons

Croutons are very easy to make at home and they can turn an ordinary salad into something gourmet. They can also be sprinkled over winter soups for an added crunch. Both the dill and the garlic-herb versions of this recipe are simple and delicious. Try using different breads such as whole wheat, rye, and sourdough.

INGREDIENTS:

1/3 cup butter (3/4 stick)
1 tsp. dill seed
1 tbsp. fresh dill weed (or 2 tsp. dried)
1 tbsp. freshly chopped chives (omit if you don't have fresh)
4-5 cups of French bread, cut into 1-inch cubes

1. Preheat oven to 350 degrees. In a small sauce pan, melt butter. Remove from heat and add the herbs. Stir well and set aside.
2. Place bread cubes in a large bowl. Drizzle one-half of the butter mixture over the bread cubes and then stir gently. Drizzle the remaining butter over the bread cubes and gently

stir again until they are well coated, but not soggy. (Different breads absorb differently, so you may not need all the butter in the recipe.)

3. Spread the buttered bread cubes, in a single layer, on an aluminum foil-lined cookie sheet. Place in the preheated oven and bake for approximately 16-20 minutes or until the cubes are crispy on both sides and slightly browned. Watch them closely so that they do not burn.

4. Remove and let cool. Store leftovers in an airtight container.

Garlic-Herb Croutons

Follow the recipe above, substituting the following for the dill and chives:

INGREDIENTS:

1 glove garlic, minced
1 tbsp. freshly chopped sage (or 2 tsp. dried)
1 tsp. freshly chopped thyme (or 1/2 tsp. dried)
1 tsp. freshly chopped parsley (or 1/2 tsp. dried)
1-2 tsp. grated Parmesan cheese (sprinkled over croutons
*   as they come out of the oven)*

YIELD: APPROXIMATELY 4–5 CUPS

Chicken Fajitas

Fajitas are very popular throughout the Southwest and are a nice change from everyday chicken recipes. They are basically just warm tortillas filled with spicy chicken, onion, and bell peppers. They are simple to make and can be served with Spanish rice, re-fried beans or a salad. Sour cream, guacamole, and salsa should be served as condiments with the fajitas. (A recipe for quick gua-camole follows.)

INGREDIENTS:

4 skinless, boneless chicken breasts
1 tbsp. vegetable oil
1/4 tsp. chili powder
1/4 tsp. ground cumin
1 onion, roughly chopped
1 red bell pepper, cut into strips
1 green bell pepper, cut into strips
2 tbsp. water
1 tbsp. freshly chopped cilantro
flour tortillas
sour cream
guacamole
medium-hot salsa

1. Cut the boneless chicken into 1-inch cubes. Heat the oil in a nonstick skillet. Add the chicken, chili powder, and cumin and sauté over a medium-high heat until the meat is fully cooked and starting to brown (about 10–12 minutes).
2. Add the onion and bell peppers to the skillet. Continue to sauté until the onions begin to brown and caramelize.
3. Add 2 tbsp. of water to the skillet. Continue to stir the fajitas for 1–2 minutes as the water deglazes the pan and creates a sauce. Add the cilantro and heat through.
4. Fill warm tortillas with the fajita mixture. Add a generous spoonful of sour cream, guacamole, and salsa to each plate. Serve immediately.

YIELD: 4 SERVINGS

Quick Guacamole

Guacamole is an avocado dip. You can serve it as a condiment with the fajitas described above or as an appetizer with tortilla chips. This guacamole is quick because you use a commercial salsa instead of homemade. This eliminates the peeling and seeding of the tomatoes and jalapenos, which can take time. Try to make this within a few hours of serving. The lemon juice will help prevent the avocados from browning, but with time the avocados begin to oxidize.

INGREDIENTS:

2 ripe avocados, peeled and pit removed
2 tbsp. fresh lemon juice
1/2 onion, finely chopped
2-4 tbsp. chunky salsa
1 tbsp. freshly chopped cilantro
salt to taste

1. Chop the avocados and place in a medium-sized bowl with the lemon juice. Use a fork to mash the avocados.
2. Add the onion, salsa, and cilantro. Mix well. Add salt to taste. Store covered in the refrigerator until ready to serve.

Roasted Rosemary Chicken with Wild Rice Stuffing

There is something very comforting about the aroma of roasted chicken on a cold winter day. This rosemary chicken can definitely be classified as a comfort food. It is tender, moist, and flavorful! The wild rice stuffing should be made ahead of time and allowed to cool before stuffing the bird. (This is to prevent bacteria from forming.) If you choose not to stuff the bird with wild rice, try filling the bird's cavity with a handful of rosemary branches and a few slices of lemon. The results will be equally delicious.

A 5–7-pound, stuffed bird will take about 2 1/2–3 1/2 hours to cook. The bird is done when the juices run clear and the leg joint moves very easily. To be safe, you may want to purchase an inexpensive instant-read thermometer. They are invaluable in the kitchen. The chicken is done when the thermometer reads 160 degrees in the thickest part of the breast.

INGREDIENTS:

5–7 lb. roasting chicken
wild rice stuffing (recipe to follow)
2 tbsp. vegetable oil
1 tbsp. freshly chopped rosemary (or 2 tsp. dried)

1. Preheat oven to 350 degrees. Remove giblets and rinse inside and outside of the bird. Pat dry with paper towels.
2. Fill the cavity of the chicken with cold, wild rice stuffing.
3. Place the bird in a shallow, medium-sized roasting pan. Brush the outside of the chicken with oil and sprinkle with the rosemary.
4. Loosely cover the chicken with aluminum foil. Roast in the preheated oven for 2 1/2–3 1/2 hours or until the juices run clear and the leg joint moves easily. (The thickest part of the

breast should register 160 degrees on a meat thermometer
when done.)
5. When the chicken is done, remove it from the oven and let
rest for 10-15 minutes before slicing.

YIELD: **4** PORTIONS

Herbal Wild Rice Stuffing

୬୨ଟ୍ଟ

This recipe makes more than enough stuffing for a 7-pound
chicken. The extra stuffing can be placed in a small casserole pan
and cooked alongside the chicken during the last 30-45 minutes
of cooking time. More than just a stuffing, this wild rice recipe can
be made anytime as a side dish too!

This recipe calls for long-grain brown rice because it has a delicious, nutty flavor. Long-grain white rice may be substituted, but
your cooking time in Step 1 may be shorter.

INGREDIENTS:

3/4 cup wild rice (rinsed)
1 1/2 cups long-grain brown rice
3 3/4 cups chicken broth
2 bay leaves (fresh or dried)
1 tbsp. olive oil
1 cup finely chopped celery
1 cup finely chopped onion
1/2 cup finely chopped leeks (white portion only)
2 cloves garlic, minced
1 tbsp. freshly chopped sage leaves (or 2 tsp. dried)
1 tbsp. freshly chopped marjoram leaves (or 1 tsp. dried)
1/4 tsp. salt
1/4 tsp. pepper

1. In a large sauce pan, combine wild rice, brown rice, chicken broth, and bay leaf. Bring to a boil, reduce heat, and cover. Simmer for 30–45 minutes or until all the liquid is absorbed by the rice.
2. Meanwhile, in a large skillet, combine oil, celery, onion, leeks, garlic, and herbs. Sauté on medium-high heat for 3–4 minutes. Stir constantly to prevent the onions and garlic from browning. (You only want to sweat the vegetables, not brown them.) Remove from heat and set aside.
3. When the rice is done cooking, remove from heat and add the sautéed vegetables. Add the salt and pepper and stir well. Set rice aside to cool completely before stuffing the chicken (or serve immediately as a side dish).

YIELD: 6–7 CUPS

Pan-Fried Red Snapper with Fennel Seed and Lemon Grass

This recipe is fast! If you mix up the herb bread crumbs ahead of time, you can bread the fish, fry it, and serve it in less than 10 minutes! And by using a nonstick frying pan, you greatly reduce the amount of oil needed. The three-step breading procedure described below is the best way to get an even crust that won't flake off while cooking. You can use the same procedure to bread other types of fish too.

You'll find that the lemon grass and fennel in this recipe create a sensational flavor combination and they do not overpower the delicate flavor of the fish. If the lemon grass is too difficult to cut with a kitchen knife, use scissors.

Since this recipe uses a nonstick skillet, only 1 tbsp. of oil is needed. If you use any other type of skillet, you may need more oil to prevent sticking.

INGREDIENTS:

4 red snapper fillets
1 cup unseasoned bread crumbs
4 tsp. finely chopped lemon grass leaves
2 tsp. fennel seed
4 tsp. dried marjoram
1/2 tsp. ground black pepper
1/2 tsp. garlic powder
1 tbsp. freshly grated lemon zest
1 cup flour
2 eggs, beaten
1 tbsp. vegetable oil
2 lemons, cut into wedges (to serve with the fish)

1. Rinse the red snapper fillets and pat dry with paper towels. Set aside.
2. In a small bowl, combine the bread crumbs, lemon grass, fennel seed, marjoram, pepper, garlic powder, and lemon zest. Mix well.
3. Place 3 plates in a row on the counter. (This is going to be your breading assembly line.) On the first plate, pour out the flour. On the second plate, pour out the beaten eggs. On the third plate, place the herbed bread crumbs.
4. Pour 1 tbsp. of vegetable oil into a nonstick frying pan and place over medium-high heat. Take one fillet and dredge it in the flour then dip it into the egg. Next, dredge it in the herb bread crumbs. (Be sure to get a thick coating of bread crumbs on the fillet.)
5. Place the breaded fillet in the hot pan and repeat the breading procedure with the remaining fillets. Pan-fry all the fish fillets over medium-high heat for approximately 3–4 minutes per side or until the outside is golden brown and center is flaky. (Depending upon the size of the skillet and the fillets, you may only be able to cook two or three at a time.)
6. Serve immediately with lemon wedges.

YIELD: 4 PORTIONS

Beef Stew with Bay and Savory

This is a rather traditional beef stew that I have made for years. For a different flavor, substitute fresh rosemary for the fresh savory. Serve this hardy meal with a crusty bread.

INGREDIENTS:

2 tbsp. vegetable oil
1 1/2 lbs. beef stew meat, cut into 1-inch cubes
1 cup flour
2 cups beef broth
1 cup tomato juice
1 15 oz. can stewed tomatoes (about 2 cups)
1 onion, roughly chopped
2 bay leaves (fresh or dried)
1 tbsp. freshly chopped savory
2 gloves garlic, pressed
1/4 tsp. ground black pepper
4 large carrots, cut into 3-inch pieces
3 stalks of celery, cut into 3-inch pieces
4 small white potatoes, cut in half
salt to taste

1. Heat the oil in a Dutch oven. Rinse the stew meat, pat it dry with paper towels, and dredge it in the flour.
2. Cook the floured meat in the oil until browned. Add beef broth, tomato juice, stewed tomatoes, onion, bay leaves, savory, pressed garlic, and black pepper. Stir and cover. Simmer over low heat for 1 hour, stirring occasionally.
3. Add carrots, celery, and white potatoes to the stew. Stir well. Cover and simmer an additional 30–45 minutes or until potatoes are fork tender.
4. Add salt to taste. Serve immediately.

YIELD: 4 SERVINGS

Roasted Potatoes with Rosemary and Oregano

These hardy potatoes are a great accompaniment to any meal. The aroma coming from the kitchen as they roast will be enough to make everyone's mouth water! This recipe serves six, but if you want to serve only four, reduce the amount of potatoes to 2 pounds. Leftovers are easily reheated the next day, either in the microwave or a low oven. When using red or white potatoes, you should leave the skin on. However, if substituting russet potatoes, peel them before roasting.

INGREDIENTS:

1/4 cup vegetable oil
2 tbsp. freshly chopped rosemary
1 tbsp. freshly chopped oregano
1/4 cup chopped scallions
1 glove garlic, minced
1/4 tsp. salt
1/4 tsp. pepper
2 1/2-3 lbs. red or white potatoes, quartered (halved if small)

1. Preheat oven to 350 degrees. In a large bowl, combine oil, herbs, scallions, garlic, salt, and pepper. Mix well.
2. Add the quartered potatoes to the oil and herb mixture. Stir well until all the potatoes are well coated.
3. Place the potatoes in a medium-sized roasting pan. Roast, uncovered, in a 350-degree oven for 45–60 minutes or until they are browned on the outside and fork tender in the center. Stir them occasionally while roasting. Serve them hot out of the oven.

YIELD: 6 SERVINGS

Garden Salad

⊱❊⊰

This garden salad is a colorful mixture of fresh flowers and greens. It is as beautiful as it is delicious. Be sure that the flowers are pesticide-free and washed thoroughly—especially nasturtiums and calendulas. (Sometimes, little insects wedge themselves down inside the petals.) Some flowers, such as borage and pansies, should be served whole. Large flowers, such as calendulas, should be separated into individual petals. (Nasturtiums can be served either way.) Blossoms from chives, hyssop, and mint should be roughly chopped.

INGREDIENTS:

4 cups mixed greens: butter lettuce, endive, and spinach leaves
1/2 cup fresh sorrel leaves
1/2 cup peeled and sliced cucumber
1/2 cup shredded carrots
2 tbsp. roughly chopped salad burnet leaves
1 tsp. finely chopped basil leaves or flowers
1 cup of edible flowers such as borage, calendula, chives, hyssop, mint, nasturtium, and pansies

1. In a large bowl, toss together the mixed greens, sorrel, cucumber, carrots, salad burnet, and basil.
2. Add the edible flowers and toss gently. Add "Honey-Dill Dressing" (*see* below) and serve immediately. You can use any salad dressing with this recipe. However, heavy, creamy dressings will coat and cover many of the pretty flowers and leaves. A light dressing would be a better choice.

Honey-Dill Dressing

INGREDIENTS:

6 tbsp. olive oil
2 tbsp. herbal vinegar (or apple cider vinegar)
1 small shallot, finely chopped
1/2 tsp. prepared mustard
1/2 tsp. honey
2 tsp. finely chopped fresh dill leaves
pinch of salt and black pepper

1. In a small bowl, combine all ingredients. Whisk until thoroughly mixed. Pour over salad and serve.

Salad Tip: You will find that you can add a variety of herbs and flowers to any plain green salad. Next time your salad needs a little sprucing up, try adding fresh basil, mint, lemon balm, chives, dill, fennel, or salad burnet leaves for flavor. Add any of the flowers listed in the garden salad recipe for color.

Vegetable Medley
with Fennel and Thyme

To make this recipe, you will need small fennel bulbs (the bottom portion of the fennel plant, minus the stalk). Unfortunately, this means that you must harvest out the entire plant. You may want to grow several crops of fennel strictly for this purpose and pick the bulbs when the plant is still fairly young. The best fennel for this recipe is Florence fennel *(Foeniculum vulgare* var. *azoricum)*. *(See* the description of fennel in Chapter 1.) If you don't want to use up your fennel crop, you can buy fennel bulbs in the vegetable section of some supermarkets. Either way, the fennel imparts a delicate anise flavor which deliciously combines with the garlic and thyme.

INGREDIENTS:

2 small fennel bulbs (or 1 large)
2 tbsp. vegetable oil
1 cup sliced carrots
1/2 onion, sliced
1 cup sliced zucchini
1 glove garlic, minced
1 tsp. fresh thyme (1/2 tsp. dried)
salt and pepper to taste

1. Julienne the fennel bulbs. (Slice into small strips.)
2. Place the oil in a large skillet, over high heat. Add the fennel, carrots, and onions. Sauté over high heat until the onion becomes translucent.
3. Add the zucchini, garlic, and thyme. Sauté for approximately 3 minutes or until the zucchini is heated through. Add salt and pepper to taste and serve.

YIELD: APPROXIMATELY 4–5 CUPS (4 SERVINGS)

Chapter 6

❦

Sweet Herbs

Although it may sound unusual to use herbs in sweet recipes, it was actually a very ordinary practice throughout history until just recently. Many old herbals and history books make mention of herbal candies, drinks and desserts. This is probaby due to the fact that up until Medieval times, sugar was extremely scarce and herbs were used as sweeteners in many recipes. Then, during the Victorian Era, when there was a renewed interest in gardening, herbs and flowers were once again popular additions to cakes, candies and pastries. A whole new set of herbal sweets were developed

There are many herbs which lend themselves to sweet recipes. Some of them, such as rosemary and basil, have the unique quality of being useful in both sweet and savory dishes. Below is a list of herbs to try in your own pastry, cookie or dessert recipes. Keep in mind that this list is only offered as a starting point for some sweet experimentation. It is in no way complete. As you expand your herbal knowledge, you will find more herbs to add to the list. Hopefully, the recipes in this chapter will provide a little inspiration for your sweet herbal journey.

Herbs to try in sweet recipes: basil, borage flowers, lavender, lemon balm, lemon verbena, mint, pineapple sage, rose, rosemary, scented geranium, sweet woodruff.

Rose Cookies

These delicate cookies taste just like shortbread and would make an excellent accompaniment to an afternoon tea! Be sure to use only roses which are completely pesticide-free. Pink, red, or yellow roses are best because their petals will add color to the finished cookie. Always taste the roses before using them because some roses have more flavor than others. Choose the roses which are the most flavorful. The rosewater is added to enhance the rose flavor. It is available at gourmet shops, health food stores, or through mail-order.

INGREDIENTS:

1/4 cup chopped fresh rose petals
1 cup sugar
3/4 cup unsalted butter, softened
1/4 tsp. salt
1 medium egg yolk
1 tbsp. rosewater
1 tsp. vanilla
1 1/2 cups all-purpose flour

1. Preheat oven to 375 degrees.
2. Pick roses (2–3 large roses should be enough) and rinse under cool water. Pull the petals off and blot dry between two tea towels. Rose petals have a very distinctive white or yellow portion at the base of the petal (where the petal joins the flower). Use scissors or your fingers to remove this portion from each petal, since it is bitter and should always be removed when cooking with roses. Chop the rose petals, measure 1/4 cup, and set aside.
3. In a medium mixing bowl, combine sugar, butter, salt, and egg yolk. Beat until creamy.
4. Add rosewater and vanilla. Mix well.

5. In a small bowl, combine rose petals and flour. Stir gently. Add this flour mixture to the sugar mixture and beat until well combined. It should resemble sticky cookie dough.
6. Line a cookie sheet with parchment paper (or use a nonstick cookie sheet). Drop rounded teaspoonfuls of dough, about 2 inches apart, onto the cookie sheets.
7. Bake for 16–20 minutes or until golden brown around the edges and firm in the center.
8. Immediately remove the cookies and let them cool on wire racks.

YIELD: APPROXIMATELY 25 COOKIES

Lavender Scones

In this recipe, dried lavender is used to infuse the liquid with its delicate flavor. Then more lavender is added to create speckles of color. This scone recipe is very versatile because you can substitute lemon verbena for the lavender to create a completely different treat! Serve these scones hot or cold with either tea or coffee. No matter how you serve them, don't forget to include generous helpings of butter and jam!

INGREDIENTS:

3/4 cup half and half
2 tbsp. dried lavender blossoms
1 3/4 cup all-purpose flour
1/4 cup sugar
1 tsp. baking soda
1/4 cup vegetable shortening
2 tsp. dried lavender
1 tbsp. sugar
1/2 tsp. ground cinnamon

1. In a small sauce pan, heat half and half until very warm (not boiling). Remove from heat and stir in the 2 tbsp. lavender. Set aside to steep for 20–30 minutes. Strain mixture and discard herbs.
2. Preheat oven to 425 degrees.
3. In a medium mixing bowl, combine flour, sugar, and baking soda. Stir to mix well.
4. Add shortening and use a pastry blender, two knives, or your fingers to cut in the shortening until the mixture resembles coarse meal.
5. Add the strained half and half and 2 tsp. dried lavender to the flour mixture. Use a fork and then your fingers to combine into a soft dough.
6. Turn the dough out onto a lightly floured surface. Form a ball and then gently roll the dough out into a 1/2-inch thick circle (about 9 inches in diameter).
7. Combine the 1 tbsp. sugar with the 1/2 tsp. cinnamon and sprinkle a light coating of this mixture over the top of the dough.
8. Place on a parchment-lined cookie sheet (or nonstick) and bake at 425 degrees for 12–15 minutes or until golden brown.
9. Remove the cookie sheet from the oven and let cool for 5 minutes. Cut the circle into eight wedges like a pizza. The scones may be eaten now or placed on a rack to cool completely. (They can also be reheated later in the microwave.)

Lemon Verbena Variation: Omit the lavender and substitute 1/4 cup whole, fresh lemon verbena leaves for the 2 tbsp. dried lavender. Add 2 tsp. grated lemon zest (the yellow portion of the peel) to the flour. Follow the remaining instructions as written.

YIELD: 8 SCONES

Lemon Verbena Strawberry Shortcake

This is a new version of an old American classic. The lemon verbena adds a nice, tart accent to the sweet strawberries. The biscuits used to create this dessert are actually quite delicious on their own. If you don't use them all for the strawberry shortcake, you can serve the leftovers with tea. They are also delicious when sprinkled with powdered sugar. Yum!

INGREDIENTS:

3/4 cup half and half
1/4 cup whole lemon verbena leaves
1 3/4 cup all-purpose flour
3 tbsp. sugar
2 tsp. baking powder
1/2 tsp. baking soda
1/4 tsp. salt
1 tbsp. lemon zest
2 tbsp. vegetable shortening
2 tbsp. butter
5 cups sliced strawberries
1/4 cup sugar
whipped cream
extra lemon verbena leaves for garnishing

1. In a small pan, heat the half and half until hot, but not boiling. Remove from heat, add lemon verbena, and let steep for 20–30 minutes. Strain mixture and discard herbs.
2. Preheat oven to 425 degrees.
3. In a medium-sized bowl, combine flour, 3 tbsp. of sugar, baking powder, baking soda, salt, and lemon zest. Mix well.
4. Add shortening and butter to the flour mixture. Use a pastry blender, two knives, or your fingers to cut the shortening

and butter into the flour until the mixture resembles coarse meal.

5. Add the half and half to the flour mixture. Use a fork and then your fingers to combine into a soft dough. Roll dough out on a floured board to 1/2 inch thick. Use a 3-inch biscuit cutter to cut out six circles. (You may have to reroll scraps to get six.)

6. Place circles on a parchment-lined (or nonstick) cookie sheet and bake at 425 degrees for 10–12 minutes or until golden brown. Place on a rack to cool.

7. When you are ready to assemble the shortcakes, mix the strawberries and the 1/4 cup sugar together in a small bowl.

8. Cut each biscuit in half horizontally. Place the bottom half on a plate, and top with a generous helping of strawberries. Place a scoop of whipped cream over the strawberries and place the biscuit top over the whipped cream.

9. Add a small dollop of whipped cream to the top of each shortcake stack and place a few lemon verbena leaves on for garnish. Serve immediately.

YIELD: 6 SHORTCAKES

Lemon Balm Tart

Colorful flakes of lemon balm create a beautiful mosaic in this pastry crust, which can be used to make all kinds of pies and tarts. The filling for this 9-inch tart is tangy and creamy. It is sure to be a hit at your next party. Serve with a sprig of lemon balm as a garnish.

CRUST:

1 1/4 cups flour
1/4 tsp. salt
2 tbsp. sugar
2 tsp. grated lemon zest (yellow portion of peel)
2 tbsp. finely chopped lemon balm leaves
1/3 cup vegetable shortening
3–4 tbsp. cold water

1. Preheat oven to 425 degrees. In a large bowl, combine flour, salt, sugar, lemon zest, and lemon balm. Stir well.
2. Add shortening and use two knives, a pastry blender, or your fingers to cut in the shortening until the mixture resembles coarse meal.
3. Add 2 tbsp. of cold water and mix with a fork until it begins to form a dough. Knead the dough with your hands. If the

dough feels too dry, add some of the remaining water, a little at a time, until a soft dough forms that holds together. (You may not need all the water.)

4. On a lightly floured board, roll out dough to a 1/8-inch thick circle. Place this circle inside a 9-inch tart pan and trim edges. Prick the bottom of crust with a fork.
5. Bake crust at 425 degrees for 13–16 minutes or until edges are a golden brown. Remove and let cool.

FILLING:

1 1/2 cups water
1/2 cup roughly chopped lemon balm leaves
4 tbsp. cornstarch
1/2 cup sugar
pinch of salt
1/3 cup freshly squeezed lemon juice
3 medium egg yolks, slightly beaten
2 tsp. lemon zest (yellow portion of peel)
2 tbsp. unsalted butter

1. In a small sauce pan, combine water and lemon balm leaves. Bring water to a boil, remove from heat, and cover. Let herbs steep 20–30 minutes. Strain mixture and discard herbs.
2. In a medium, heavy-bottomed sauce pan, whisk together strained water, cornstarch, sugar, and salt. Bring mixture to a boil, stirring constantly. Boil for 1 minute.
3. Remove pan from heat and stir in lemon juice. Pour a small amount of this hot cornstarch mixture into the beaten egg yolks. Stir well. Then, pour the egg yolks back into the cornstarch mixture and stir well. Return the pan to the stove.
4. Bring mixture to a simmer and cook for 4 minutes over medium-low heat or until an instant-read thermometer reads at least 165 degrees for 1 minute. Stir constantly so mixture does not burn.

5. Remove the pan from the heat and stir in lemon zest and butter. Stir until butter is melted and completely incorporated. Pour the finished lemon filling into the baked tart shell. Let cool completely before serving. Store any leftovers in the refrigerator.

YIELD: ONE 9-INCH LEMON TART

Open-Faced Rosemary-Apple Pie

This pie recipe makes a very unusual presentation and your guests will have trouble distinguishing the secret ingredient—rosemary. It adds a wonderfully subtle flavor which, when combined with the marmalade, makes a very delicious accent. If you don't want to take the time to make your own pie crust, a ready-made or a boxed crust will work almost as well. Just hide the box so your guests won't know!

CRUST:

1 1/4 cups all-purpose flour
1/4 tsp. salt
2 tbsp. sugar
1/3 cup vegetable shortening
3-4 tbsp. cold water

1. In a medium-sized bowl, combine flour, salt, and sugar. Mix well.
2. Add shortening and use two knives, a pastry blender, or your fingers to cut in the shortening until the mixture resembles coarse meal.
3. Add 2 tbsp. of cold water and mix with a fork until it begins to form a dough. Knead the dough with your hands. If dough

feels too dry, add some of the remaining water, a little at a time, until a soft dough forms that holds together. (You may not need all the water.)

4. On a lightly floured board, roll out dough into a 1/8-inch-thick circle. Place on a parchment-lined (or nonstick) cookie sheet and cover with a piece of plastic wrap. Set in the refrigerator until filling is ready.

FILLING:

5-6 Granny Smith apples
juice of 1 lemon
1 tsp. vanilla
2 tsp. chopped rosemary leaves
3 tbsp. sugar
1 tsp. cinnamon
1/2 tsp. allspice
1 tsp. cornstarch
4 tbsp. orange or lemon marmalade
1-2 tbsp. butter
aluminum foil

1. Preheat oven to 400 degrees.
2. Peel, core, and slice apples and place in a mixing bowl with the lemon juice. Add vanilla and stir apples well to coat.
3. In a small bowl, combine sugar, cinnamon, allspice, and cornstarch. Sprinkle over apples and mix well.
4. Remove the rolled-out crust from the refrigerator and remove plastic wrap. Place the marmalade in the center of the crust and spread evenly to within 2 inches of the edge. Carefully place a layer of apple slices in a spiral pattern, starting at the center of the crust and stopping 2 inches from the edge. Continue placing spiral layers until all apples have been used.
5. Fold the crust edges over twice and roll up over the edge of the apples. If necessary, place rolled strips of aluminum foil around the edges to hold crust in place.

6. Pour any remaining juice from the apple mixture into the center of the pie and dot the apples with pieces of the remaining tablespoon of butter. Bake at 400 degrees for 40–45 minutes. (Remove foil during last 5 minutes.) Serve warm or cold with whipped cream.

YIELD: 1 PIE

Chocolate Mint Pudding

Don't let the thought of making chocolate pudding from scratch intimidate you. It is incredibly easy and sinfully delicious! You'll be amazed at how creamy, minty, and rich the final product is! Tremendously better than any store-bought pudding, this dessert is sure to satisfy any chocoholic! If you don't have spearmint, fresh peppermint leaves may be substituted.

INGREDIENTS:

2 cups milk
1 cup roughly chopped, fresh spearmint leaves
3 oz. semisweet chocolate
1 oz. unsweetened chocolate
1/2 cup sugar
pinch of salt
2 tbsp. cornstarch
2 medium egg yolks, slightly beaten
1 tsp. vanilla
1 tbsp. butter, cut into pieces
extra mint sprig for garnishing

1. In a small sauce pan, combine milk and spearmint. Heat over a medium flame until milk is very hot, but not boiling. Remove from heat, cover, and set aside for 20 minutes. Strain

mixture and discard mint. Remove approx. 1/2 cup of the milk and set aside.

2. Melt the chocolate in the top half of a double boiler, stirring occasionally.

3. In a large sauce pan with a heavy bottom, combine melted chocolate with only 1 1/2 cups of the mint-flavored milk. Whisk or stir vigorously to combine. (Do not be concerned if the chocolate creates small flakes; they will melt later.)

4. Place the pan over medium heat and add sugar and salt. Bring to a boil.

5. In a separate bowl, combine the cornstarch with the reserved 1/2 cup mint-milk mixture. Mix well. Pour this into the chocolate mixture and return to a boil, stirring constantly. (Be careful not to burn the bottom; lower heat if necessary.) The chocolate mixture will thicken considerably after boiling for about 30–60 seconds. When this happens, remove from heat.

6. Pour a small amount of the chocolate mixture into the slightly beaten egg yolks. Mix well and then pour the yolks back into the chocolate. Return the pan to the stove and cook over a medium-low flame for 3 minutes, stirring constantly.

7. Remove from heat and stir in vanilla and butter. Stir well until the butter melts and is well incorporated. (The pudding will continue to thicken as it cools.) Pour pudding into 4–5 half-cup serving dishes and let cool. Serve with fresh mint sprigs as garnishes.

YIELD: 4–5 HALF-CUP SERVINGS

Basil-Lemon Sorbet

This light dessert is the perfect finish to a spicy meal! The coolness of this icy white sorbet with its lemonade flavor is very refreshing, and the hint of basil makes it very exotic. The lemon zest is included for extra flavor.

INGREDIENTS:

2 cups water
1 cup sugar
1/2 cup roughly chopped fresh basil leaves
1/3 cup freshly squeezed lemon juice
1/2 tsp. lemon zest (yellow portion of the peel)

1. In a small sauce pan, bring the water and sugar to a hard boil. Stir for 1 minute and then add the basil. Remove from heat, cover, and let mixture sit for 20 minutes.
2. Strain the basil water into a bowl and set aside to cool completely. (Placing it in the refrigerator will speed up the cooling process.)
3. Add lemon juice and zest. Stir well.
4. Pour into your ice cream maker and freeze according to the manufacturer's instructions.
5. Store in the freezer, but place sorbet in the refrigerator 15 minutes before serving to soften. Eat within 1 week.

YIELD: APPROXIMATELY 2 CUPS

Rosemary-Orange Sorbet

This sorbet recipe is very unusual and very delicious. The combination of rosemary and orange complement each other very well and create a flavorful summertime treat. Use freshly squeezed orange juice if possible. Try serving small scoops of this sorbet in wineglasses with a sprig of fresh rosemary as a garnish. Very elegant!

INGREDIENTS:

2 cups water
1/2 cup sugar
1 tbsp. roughly chopped, fresh rosemary leaves
1 cup orange juice
1 tsp. orange zest (the orange portion of the peel)

1. In a small sauce pan, bring the water and sugar to a hard boil. Stir for 1 minute and then add the rosemary. Remove from heat, cover, and let sit for 15 minutes.
2. Strain the rosemary water into a bowl and set aside to cool completely. (Placing it in the refrigerator will speed up the cooling process.)
3. Add the orange juice and zest. Stir well.
4. Pour into your ice cream maker and freeze according to the manufacturer's instructions.
5. Store in the freezer but place sorbet in the refrigerator 15 minutes before serving to soften. Eat within 1 week.

YIELD: APPROXIMATELY 2 CUPS

Minty Fruit Salad

For a quick and easy lunchtime treat, try this refreshing mint and fruit salad. You can use peppermint, spearmint, or apple mint to get a variety of flavors. If your mint is blooming, try adding chopped mint blossoms to the salad for extra flavor and color. The advantage of using the concentrated apple juice is that it eliminates the need for sugar. Any combination of fruit is delicious in this salad. Add the fruits you prefer or have in season.

INGREDIENTS:

1/2 cup frozen apple juice concentrate
1/4 cup chopped fresh mint leaves
1/2 cantaloupe, cut into 1-inch cubes (about 5-6 cups)
1/2 honeydew melon, cut into 1-inch cubes (about 5-6 cups)
1 cup seedless grapes
1 tsp. freshly chopped mint leaves

1. In a small sauce pan, combine apple juice and 1/4 cup mint leaves. Bring to a boil, remove from heat, and set aside to cool. Strain.
2. In a large bowl, combine fruit and 1 tsp. freshly chopped mint. Pour half the apple juice mixture over the fruit and stir well. Taste and add more juice to sweeten if necessary. Serve immediately.

Pineapple Sage Variation: For a different twist on this simple salad, try substituting fresh pineapple sage for the mint. Be sure to include some fresh pineapple in the mixed fruit!

YIELD: APPROXIMATELY 2 1/2–3 QUARTS (DEPENDING UPON FRUIT USED)

Herbs in the Home

Beginning in sixteenth-century Europe, many homes had a "stillroom," where the housewife or maid concocted herbal medicines, soaps, cordials, tinctures, and aromatics for the home. It was usually next to the kitchen, and had its own fire and still for distilling important potions such as lavender oil or rosewater. It was from here that all the preparations were developed to keep the household clean, fragrant, and healthy. Many of these women kept stringent notes on how to create these recipes in stillroom books, which were passed down through generations.

Luckily for us, it is no longer necessary to have a special room to distill essential oils and create fragrant potions. But that doesn't make the thought of recreating some of those old recipes any less romantic. Many of the concoctions of the past can be adapted for modern purposes. For example, in Medieval times, herbs were strewn all over the floor so that their scent would be released when stepped upon. Although herb strewing is impractical today, herb powders can be sprinkled over carpeting and vacuumed up to achieve the same effect. Some of the old stillroom recipes for cosmetics can be easily recreated today by using just a few fresh ingredients right out of the garden and kitchen.

Historically, herbs have also been used in the home as decorations. It was an ancient practice to bring the fragrances of the garden indoors through freshly cut flowers and herbs. But herbs have other decorative qualities as well. They can be pressed flat and dried to be used in a variety of whimsical designs and decorations. They can even be used to decorate gift wrap!

Many people are familiar with the culinary aspects of herbs. But it is fascinating to explore the soothing, fragrant, and decorative history of herbs and how these attributes can be adapted to our modern way of living. This section focuses on some of these herbal characteristics and how we can use them in our own homes.

Chapter 7

৵৩৵৹৵

Beauty from the Garden: Herbal Cosmetics

Throughout recorded history, there is evidence that people all over the world created botanical cosmetics for both beauty and fragrance. The early Egyptians used ointments and perfumes for personal adornment and ancient rituals. The Romans used herbs in skin preparations and fragrant baths. During the sixteenth and seventeenth centuries, most well-to-do Europeans had a stillroom in their household, where essential oils were distilled from plants and used to create colognes, bath waters, and pomades (a perfumed ointment for the hair or scalp). In Colonial America, women grew herbs outside their kitchen doors for many purposes including beauty products. They made soaps, perfumes, lotions, and room deodorizers. But the romance of homemade cosmetics is probably best captured by the Victorian women, who would whisper beauty secrets to each other over afternoon tea or write of fragrant concoctions in their private journals.

Many of these old-time botanical toiletries and fragrances have been handed down through generations by mothers, daughters, alchemists, midwives, and house servants. Today, we can combine the best of this historical knowledge with today's technology to create our own personalized, all-natural beauty potions.

It can be very nostalgic to gather fragrant ingredients from the garden to make old-fashioned toiletries. But there are also some great advantages to creating your own homemade cosmetics:

1. You are guaranteed that everything is fresh and preservative-free.
2. You can choose ingredients specifically geared for your own skin and hair type.
3. You can personalize them by using your favorite essential oils for fragrance.
4. You can present them as gifts in creative packaging with the recipe attached.

INGREDIENTS AND WHERE TO FIND THEM

Some of the ingredients listed in the following recipes may sound a bit exotic, but most can be found in your local supermarket, pharmacy, health food store, or your own herb garden. What you can't find locally can be ordered from some of the mail-order companies listed in the "Source Guide" at the back of this book. (Dried herbs such as chamomile and calendula can sometimes be found in the "bulk tea" section at the health food store.)

Almond Oil, Sweet: This makes an excellent all-purpose body oil because it is very emollient. Look for it in health food stores, in some grocery stores, or from one of the mail-order sources listed in this book.

Aloe Vera Gel: This is the sap from the aloe vera plant, which has antifungal and moisturizing properties. Aloe has a long history of medicinal uses including soothing dry, irritated, or burned skin. It can be found at some pharmacies, in health food stores, or through mail-order sources.

Apricot Kernel Oil: This oil can be found in health food stores, in some supermarkets, and through mail-order. It is a light oil which soaks into the skin well.

Beeswax: When used in conjunction with borax, beeswax acts as an emulsifying agent in cosmetics. It also gives a protective layer to the skin and holds in moisture. It can be found in many health food stores, candle supply houses, beekeeping stores, or one of the sources listed in the "Source Guide." I prefer to use pure, unbleached beeswax, which has a brown color and a sweet, honey scent. Some people like the bleached beeswax "pearls" or "beads" because they are easier to measure. If you wish to use them, be sure they do not have other additives. Beeswax has a very long shelf life and will not turn rancid.

Borax Powder (Sodium borate): This naturally occurring mineral is a water softener and can be found in the detergent section of the supermarket. In cosmetics it is used as an emulsifier, stabilizer, and preservative. It is only mildly alkaline so it can be helpful in cleaning the skin without drying it out.

Castor Oil: Castor oil is a heavy, emollient oil which can be used in a variety of cosmetic recipes. It can act as a fixative in colognes because it dissolves readily in alcohol and then helps slow evaporation of the volatile oils after it is applied to the skin. It can be found in the health food section of supermarkets, in health food stores, in pharmacies, and through mail-order.

Cream of Tartar: This is a by-product left after the fermentation of grapes into wine. It is an acid which is used in baking to stabilize beaten egg whites, among other things. It is used in some foot bath recipes in combination with baking soda to create an effervescence. Cream of tartar can be found in the spice section of the supermarket. If you can't find it, tartaric acid, which is at your local pharmacy, may be used in foot baths.

Essential Oils: The term "essential oil" is used throughout this book. It is important to understand that there is a big difference between an "essential" oil and a "fragrance" or "craft" oil. An essential oil is the volatile oil of a plant. It holds the fragrance and other properties of that plant which are valuable for culinary and therapeutic uses. The essential oil is stored in different areas of the plant, depending upon the plant variety. The extraction can be very labor-intensive and, therefore, a very expensive process.

A "fragrance" or "craft" oil is a cheaper, synthetic version of an essential oil. It may have a similar fragrance, but it does not possess the same therapeutic properties. It is *not* recommended that you use *any* synthetic oils or synthetic ingredients in homemade cosmetics. Not only will they lack the deep aromas and characteristics of pure essential oils, they may also cause allergic reactions to the skin. (Some pure essential oils can cause skin irritations as well. *See* "Allergic Reactions," below.) Sources for reputable pure essential oils are given in the "Source Guide" at the back of this book. They can also be found at some health food stores.

Glycerine: This thick, clear liquid occurs in the fat of most animals and vegetables in combination with fatty acids. It is a very common ingredient in commercial cosmetics because it is able to hold moisture against the surface of the skin and helps prevent drying. It mixes well with water and dissolves in alcohol. It can be found at pharmacies and through mail-order.

Grapeseed Oil: This oil is a bit more expensive but is far less greasy than other oils. It is very good for delicate, sensitive skin. It can be found in some health food stores or through mail-order.

Jojoba Bean Oil: This oil is terrific in body products because it is very similar to the skin's naturally secreted oils. It can be found at most health food stores or through mail-order.

Oatmeal: This morning cereal actually makes a wonderful cosmetic ingredient! It has mild cleansing properties and is beneficial to dry, sensitive skin. Be sure to buy the old-fashioned oats in the cereal section of the supermarket, not "quick-cooking" oats.

Sunflower Oil: This is a light and inexpensive oil which can be found in most health food stores and supermarkets and through mail-order.

Tincture of Benzoin: Tincture of benzoin is an alcohol-based product made from a gum resin secreted from the *Styrax benzoin* tree. It can usually be found in the antibacterial section of the pharmacy. You can also create your own by ordering Gum Benzoin *(Styrax benzoin)* through the mail and making a tincture using grain alcohol or vodka. *(See* "tinctures" in the terminology section of this chapter.) It is used in cosmetics as a preservative.

EQUIPMENT

There is really no special equipment required other than standard kitchen items such as pots, pans, and measuring tools. It is best to use stainless steel, enamel, or glass when making cosmetics to prevent a chemical reaction. Wash all equipment and storage containers in hot soapy water before using to make sure that everything is immaculately clean. (Any bacteria on your equipment will cause your cosmetics to prematurely spoil.)

Allergic Reactions

Most of the commercial cosmetics on the market today are made with synthetics and preservatives which can be very irritating to people with sensitive skin. Although homemade cosmetics are free from synthetics and preservatives, there is still the possibility of an allergic reaction to a particular herb or other ingredient. If you have sensitive skin or are worried about allergies, it is wise to do a patch test on each new cosmetic before spreading it all over your face or body. Once a particular sensitivity is known, that ingredient can be avoided, allowing your homemade creations to be problem-free.

PATCH TEST

Patch Test for Homemade Cosmetics: Place a small amount of the cosmetic mixture onto the inside crease of your arm and cover it with a Band-Aid. Wait 24 hours. If you have no reaction, then the cosmetic is safe to use. However, if you have any redness, hives, or swelling, then you are allergic and should avoid that mixture!

Patch Test for Just Herbs: Chop approximately 1 teaspoon of the herb in question and mix it with a small amount of plain water. Place this mixture onto the inside crease of your arm. Cover with a 100% cotton ball and a Band-Aid to hold in place. Leave the patch on for 24 hours. Remove the patch and check for a reaction. If you see no reaction, then the herb is safe to use.

PRESERVATIVES

Some of the ingredients in homemade cosmetics such as tincture of benzoin or alcohol have preservative properties and can help prolong the life of your mixtures. However, none of the recipes will last as long as commercial cosmetics. Try to use up your mixtures within a few months unless otherwise advised in the recipe. Lotions and creams have a longer shelf life if stored in the refrigerator. Colognes, bath bags, and bath oils can be stored on a shelf or in a dark cupboard away from direct sunlight. If you ever notice a bad smell coming from one of your mixtures, it has probably spoiled and should be discarded.

FIXATIVES

Fixatives are used in perfumery and potpourri making. They "fix" or hold the fragrance and make it long-lasting. Castor oil, tincture of benzoin, and glycerine can be used in cosmetics as fixatives. Some essential oils such as sandalwood and patchouli also have this property.

TERMINOLOGY

TINCTURES

A *tincture* is the result of steeping plant material in a solvent (usually alcohol or vinegar) to extract the essential elements of that particular plant. The mixture is a concentrated form of the plant's key elements, which can then be easily added to cosmetics. To make a tincture, the solvent is usually heated and the plant material is added and allowed to steep. Then the mixture is strained and bottled for later use. Although this method is similar to making a tea, the tincture is more concentrated because the alcohol is able to dissolve and hold more of the plant's compounds than just water alone.

INFUSION

An *infusion* is the result of steeping plant material in plain hot water (like tea). An infusion is not as concentrated as a tincture but does contain some of the essential elements of the plant material. It can be used in hair rinses, colognes, and toilet waters.

BAIN-MARIE

Bain-marie is a fancy term for a hot water bath which is a cooking method used to heat ingredients slowly. In cosmetics, a bain-marie refers to a pan of water on a stove which has a bowl sitting on top of it. The water in the pan is brought to a simmer and the cosmetic ingredients are placed in the bowl. The steam from the pan gently heats the bowl and prevents the ingredients from overheating. A double boiler is a type of bain-marie.

PERFUMES, COLOGNES, AND TOILET WATERS

Many of the old herbals use the terms *perfume, cologne,* and *toilet water* interchangeably. However, by today's standards, there are differences. A perfume has a strong fragrance and usually contains up to 30% aromatic oil. It is very concentrated and is only dabbed on the skin in small quantities. A homemade perfume can be very costly to make, so this chapter will cover less-expensive body fragrances: i.e., colognes and toilet waters.

A cologne has a softer fragrance than perfume and only contains 1–5% aromatic oil. It usually contains alcohol but may also contain water or oil. Cologne can be used like a perfume, added to bath water, or used as a body splash after a shower.

A toilet water is even lighter in fragrance than a cologne and usually consists of an herbal infusion (herbs brewed in hot water, like tea). It is almost always used as a body splash and is expected to impart softening qualities to the skin.

Most homemade colognes and toilet waters contain some

amount of alcohol to help preserve the mixture. Alcohol also increases evaporation when it is applied to the skin. It is through this evaporation that the fragrance molecules enter the air and allow the essences to be detected by the nose. Unfortunately, recipes with large amounts of alcohol can be very drying to the skin. To counter this dryness, a small amount of glycerine or oil is usually included in the recipes.

Gardener's Hand Salve

Our hands are exposed to more harsh elements than any other part of our body, and yet, most of us neglect them completely. Gardeners should be especially careful with their hands because garden activities can expose them to cuts, scrapes, bacteria, and infection. Many of the ingredients in this salve (calendula, aloe vera, and tea tree oil) can be very helpful in healing and preventing these problems.

Calendula *(Calendula officinalis)* is very healing and is known for its anti-inflammatory and antibacterial properties. Aloe vera has anti-inflammatory and moisturizing properties and tea tree essential oil *(Melaleuca alternifolia)* is extremely antiseptic. These components combine to form this very healing salve. Just smooth it on your hands at night after a long day in the garden.

INGREDIENTS:

1/4 cup sweet almond oil
1 tbsp. dried calendula flowers
4 tsp. grated or finely chopped beeswax
6 drops tea tree essential oil
1 tsp. aloe vera gel
1/8 tsp. tincture of benzoin

1. Heat oil in a pan over a low flame until just warm. Remove from heat and add calendula flowers. Stir well, cover pan, and sit aside for 2 hours.

2. Strain out flowers and pour oil into a double boiler or bain-marie. Add beeswax. Heat the oil mixture while stirring constantly until the wax is completely melted. Immediately remove from heat and stir in tea tree essential oil.
3. Pour warm oil mixture into a mixing bowl. Add the aloe vera and tincture of benzoin. Use a whisk or electric mixer to beat the mixture vigorously until well blended (about 3 minutes).
4. Pour into a clean container with a tight-fitting lid. Set aside to cool. Store in the refrigerator and use within 3 months.

YIELD: APPROXIMATELY 2 OZ.

Chamomile Moisturizing Lotion

Chamomile has wonderful soothing and anti-inflammatory properties. To reap the benefits of this healing herb, this recipe combines a chamomile infusion with moisturizing oils to create a lotion that is very beneficial to sensitive or dry skin.

Of the three possible oils you can use in this lotion, grapeseed oil is the least greasy. It just vanishes into the skin!

INGREDIENTS:

1/3 cup distilled water
2 chamomile tea bags or 2 tsp. dried chamomile flowers
1/4 tsp. borax powder
1/2 cup sweet almond oil, grapeseed oil, or sunflower oil
1 tbsp. grated or finely chopped beeswax
8 drops roman chamomile essential oil, lemon essential oil,
  or other favorite essential oil

1. In a small pan, heat the distilled water to almost boiling. Add the chamomile and set aside for about 10 minutes.
2. Strain out the chamomile and add the borax powder. Reheat the water over a low flame until the borax is completely dissolved (about 1 minute). Remove from heat and set aside.

3. In a double boiler or bain-marie, combine oil and beeswax. Heat the oil mixture while stirring constantly until the wax is completely melted. Immediately remove from heat and stir in essential oil.
4. Pour warm oil into a mixing bowl. Use a whisk or an electric mixer to beat oil while slowly adding the warm water mixture. Beat the entire mixture for about 2 minutes.
5. Pour into a clean container, label, and store in a cool, dark place. Use within 5 months.

YIELD: APPROXIMATELY 6 OZ.

HOW IT WORKS . . .

A lotion or a cream is actually an emulsion: a mixture of oil and water which is stabilized so that it will not separate. As the oil and water mixture is beaten, tiny droplets of one liquid are dispersed throughout the other liquid. Under normal circumstances, oil and water repel each other and will eventually separate with the oil on top, water on the bottom. However, if an emulsifying agent such as borax or wax is added, the tiny droplets are coated and no longer repel the other liquid. The emulsion is formed and retains its mixed state for long periods of time.

Moisturizing Hand and Body Cream

This moisturizing cream is nongreasy and very versatile. You can use sweet almond oil, apricot kernel oil, or jojoba oil to create a very luxurious mixture. The aloe vera gel in this recipe makes the cream extremely soothing to the skin. Unfortunately, the addition of fresh aloe also requires this cream to be kept in the refrigerator. You will find that the chilled cream is actually quite refreshing! However, if you wish, you may substitute 2 tablespoons of water for the 2 tablespoons of aloe gel. The resulting cream is almost as nice and does not need to be refrigerated.

INGREDIENTS:

1/4 tsp. borax powder
2 tbsp. aloe vera gel
2 tbsp. distilled water
5 tbsp. sweet almond oil, apricot kernel oil, or jojoba oil
2 tsp. grated or finely chopped beeswax
10 drops lavender essential oil

1. In a small pan, combine the borax, aloe, and water. Heat gently until the borax is dissolved. Set aside.
2. In a double boiler or bain-marie, combine the oil and beeswax. Heat the oil mixture while stirring constantly until the wax is melted. Immediately remove from heat and stir in the lavender oil.
3. Pour the warm oil into a mixing bowl. Use a whisk or an electric mixer to beat the oil while slowly adding the warm water mixture. Beat the entire mixture for about 2 minutes.
4. Pour into a clean container with a tight-fitting lid. Label and store in the refrigerator. Use within 30 days. (If the aloe vera gel was omitted, the cream may be stored in a cool, dark place and used within 3–4 months.)

YIELD: APPROXIMATELY 4 OZ.

Lavender Cologne

Lavender, with its sweet and refreshing fragrance, has always been considered a valuable herb throughout history. Among the many royals who fancied lavender, Queen Elizabeth I of England was one of the most enthusiastic. She drank large amounts of lavender tea and spent exorbitant amounts of money on lavender perfume. She even commanded that her royal gardeners provide freshly cut lavender flowers, at a moment's notice, every day of the year! Not an easy task!

Although it may not be practical to expect fresh lavender blossoms every day, this cologne captures the essence of those lavender blossoms in a tincture which can be enjoyed anytime. Be sure to make more than one batch and give it as a gift to a special friend!

INGREDIENTS:

1/2 cup vodka
2 tbsp. dried lavender blossoms
12 drops lavender essential oil
1/4 tsp. castor oil

1. Place vodka in a glass jar and add dried lavender. Cover and let sit for 1 week.
2. After 1 week, strain out the lavender and add the essential oil and caster oil to the vodka. Cover the jar and shake vigorously.
3. Pour the cologne into a decorative jar. The cologne does not need to be refrigerated, but be sure to store it out of direct sunlight. Always shake mixture before using and use within 6 months.

YIELD: 4 OZ. COLOGNE

Victorian Toilet Water

For this old-time recipe, an herbal infusion is created using either the robust pine scent of rosemary, the cooling fragrance of lemon verbena, or the delicate perfume of rose-scented geraniums. Any one of these herbs helps create this lightly scented toilet water which can be used as a refreshing body splash after bathing.

INGREDIENTS:

1/2 cup fresh herb leaves (or 1/4 cup dried)
1 cup distilled water
1/4 cup vodka
1 tbsp. glycerine

1. Gather 1/2 cup fresh leaves of either rosemary, lemon verbena, or scented geranium from the garden (or substitute 1/4 cup dried).
2. In a small pan, heat the water to a boil.
3. Remove from heat and add the herb leaves. Stir, cover, and set aside for 1 hour.
4. Strain the herb infusion and add vodka and glycerine. Stir well.
5. Pour into a decorative bottle. Store in the refrigerator and use within 1 month.

YIELD: 12 oz.

Sweet perfumes work immediately upon the spirits for their refreshing, sweet and healthful ayres are special preservatives to health and therefore much to be praised.

—TREATISE OF FRUITE-TREES, 1653

Herbal Body Spritz

An herbal body spritz is a very easy way to revive your neglected skin throughout the day. Simply combine distilled water and essential herbal oil in a plastic spray bottle. Spritz your face, arms, and legs whenever you need a refreshing "wake-up call." The water will help moisturize your skin while the essential oil will impart some of its therapeutic components.

On hot summer days, keep a bottle of peppermint-scented

spritz in the refrigerator. Whenever the heat of the day gets to you, cool down with an aromatic misting. Keep a small 2 oz. bottle of lavender-scented spritz in your purse to soothe and refresh your skin throughout the work day.

Choose an essential oil from the list below and enjoy!

Essential Oils to Try:

Lavender *(Lavandula officinalis):* Very soothing.
Peppermint *(Mentha x piperita):* Has a cooling effect on the body.
Rose *(Rosa* spp.): Extremely expensive but very good for dry, sensitive skin.
Spearmint *(Mentha spicata):* Nice for irritated skin.

INGREDIENTS:

1 cup distilled water
10-12 drops of your favorite essential oil

Combine ingredients in a plastic spray bottle. Shake vigorously before each use. Spray the body spritz on your face, arms, and legs anytime you need a refreshing pick-me-up. The spritz does not need to be refrigerated. Use within 6 months.

YIELD: 1 CUP BODY SPRITZ.

Effervescent Foot Bath

In water, baking soda acts as a water softener and skin soother. When combined with an acid (in this case, cream of tartar), it creates carbon dioxide, which will fizzle away the stresses of the day. The carbon dioxide also helps release the peppermint oil into the air, which acts as another stress reliever. The herbs in this recipe will create an infusion in the bath water, thereby releasing their therapeutic properties. Use dried sage for aching muscles or lemon balm to cool your tired feet.

INGREDIENTS:

1/2 cup baking soda
1/2 cup cream of tartar (or tartaric acid)
6 drops peppermint essential oil
4 tbsp. dried sage or lemon balm

1. In a small bowl combine all ingredients and mix well. This mixture can be stored in an airtight jar for later use (or gift) or it can be used immediately.
2. To make a foot bath: Pour the dry bath mixture into a large owl. Add approximately 8–10 cups warm (not hot) water. Stir vigorously and immediately submerge your feet in the warm bath water. The foot bath will fizz for several minutes as the mixture dissolves. Soak feet for 10 minutes and then rinse.
3. Apply a moisturizing lotion to your feet and put on a pair of cotton socks. Your feet will love you for it!

YIELD: 1 FOOT BATH

S*weet* B*ath* B*ags*

It may sound romantic to sprinkle herbs and flowers into your bath water, but it is not recommended. What doesn't stick to your body will probably clog up your drain! A sweet bath bag is an old-fashioned solution to this dilemma. An herb-filled bag is tied onto the bathtub spout so that as the tub is filled, the bath water flows through the bag, releasing the skin softening properties. While in the bath, you can use the bag as a washcloth, which will further release the soothing components.

You can personalize the mixture by choosing your favorite herb from the list below. The oatmeal and borax are included to soothe dry skin and soften the water. This recipe is so easy to make that you may want to prepare several batches at once. Keep the filled bags inside airtight jars until ready to use. (They make thoughtful gifts too.)

There are several things you can use to "bag" up this mixture:

1. You can sew sachet bags from 6-inch by 8-inch pieces of 100% cotton fabric. Just fold the fabric lengthwise with right sides together. (It will then be 8 × 3.) Stitch one of the 3 inch sides and the open 8 inch side. Leave the other 3 inch side open. It will be the top of the bag. Turn inside out and fill with your potpourri mixture. Tie the filled bath bags with ribbon or cotton string.
2. You can purchase large muslin "tea bags" from a health food store or one of the mail-order sources listed in this book. The "tea bags" should be 100% cotton and have draw-string ties.
3. You can use antique handkerchiefs! Just place the mixture in the center and tie closed with ribbon to form sachets.
4. Cut 10 inch circles from cotton fabric. Place 1/4 cup of mixture in the center and tie with ribbon.

INGREDIENTS:

1/2 cup borax
1/2 cup dried herbs (see Step 1 below*)*
2 cups oatmeal

1. Choose the herb you wish to use in the bath bag. Use rosemary or sage for a stimulating and invigorating bath. Use

chamomile or lavender blossoms for a calming and relaxing bath.

2. Combine all ingredients in a small bowl and stir well.

3. Place 1/4–1/2 cup of the mixture into each bag or handkerchief and tie securely.

YIELD: 6–12 BATH BAGS

"Garden-Fresh" Scented Bath Oil

This bath oil is one of the most luxurious gifts you can make for yourself or a friend! The dried flowers add color and elegance, the base oil nourishes and pampers the skin, and the fragrant essential oils soothe the spirit. It is important that the flowers and spices used are completely dry. Any moisture will make the final bath oil cloudy. If you choose to use rose buds or rose petals, choose light-colored flowers. Deep colors such as red tend to turn black when dried.

The spices listed are more for show than for fragrance. Choose the ones you have available. The sweet almond oil makes an excellent base oil. The jojoba oil can add more nourishing properties to the bath oil, but is not necessary. If it is difficult to find, simply substitute more almond oil in its place.

INGREDIENTS:

dried flowers and herbs such as: lavender, larkspur, love-in-a-mist, globe amaranth, lemon verbena, miniature rose buds, rose petals, calendula petals, etc.
1 cinnamon stick
4 whole allspice (optional)
2 whole star anise (optional)
6 oz. glass bottle
4 oz. sweet almond oil

2 oz. jojoba oil (optional)
10 drops lavender essential oil
5 drops lemon or orange essential oil
raffia or ribbon for decoration

1. Place sprigs of the dried herbs and flowers inside the clean 6 oz. bottle. They will add color as well as some fragrance to the final product. Break the cinnamon stick in half and add it to the bottle. Add the other spices to the bottle if you choose to use them.
2. In a clean bowl, combine the almond oil, jojoba, and essential oils. Stir well. Using a funnel, pour the oil mixture into the bottle until full. Tie the top with raffia or ribbon.
3. Let the mixture sit for 1 week to allow the scents to blend. To use: add 1–2 tbsp. of the bath oil to your bath water for soft and supple skin.

YIELD: 6 OZ.

FOR TIRED, PUFFY EYES . . .

Chamomile has wonderful anti-inflammatory properties! Take two chamomile tea bags, dip them in cool water, and squeeze out the excess. Lie down and place one tea bag over each eye. Relax for 10 minutes.

Rose-Scented Facial Steam

Victorian women had a real love affair with roses. They were valued not only for their unequaled beauty, but for their fragrance, flavor, and medicinal uses as well. During the Victorian Era, the nighttime ritual of steaming the face with rose-scented water was very popular. This old-fashioned method is actually very efficient at cleansing the pores and softening the skin. Be sure to deeply inhale the rose fragrance as it can be very soothing and relaxing at the end of the day.

For variety, you can substitute one of the herbs listed below for the rose petals and scented geranium leaves.

Note: If you have very sensitive skin or tiny spider veins on your skin, it is *not* recommended that you ever use a facial steam.

INGREDIENTS:

1 1/2 cups fresh rose petals
1/2 cup fresh rose-scented geranium leaves
8 cups distilled water

1. Wash your face with a mild cleanser and pat dry.
2. In a large pan, bring the water almost to a boil and then remove from heat. Add rose petals and scented geranium leaves and stir well.
3. Set the pan on top of a towel on a sturdy surface. Hold your face over the steaming pan and use a towel to make a tent over your head to catch the steam. Keep your eyes closed and your face at least 10 inches away from the water's surface to prevent burning.
4. Inhale deeply and sit quietly for 6–8 minutes.
5. Rinse your face several times with cool water. Pat dry and apply a moisturizer.

Other herbs can be used in a facial steam. Try one of these or a combination! You will need approximately 1–2 cups of loosely packed fresh herbs to 8 cups of distilled water.

Chamomile: *Healing and soothing.*
Fennel leaves: *Astringent.*

Peppermint: *Cooling and refreshing.*
Rosemary: *Healing and stimulating.*

YIELD: 1 FACIAL STEAM

Herbal Hair Rinse

An herbal hair rinse is one of the easiest beauty products to make! Basically, it is just a cold herbal tea (an infusion) which is used as the final rinse after you shampoo. It does not remove tangles, but can add shine and luster to your hair.

Choose the appropriate herb from the following:

Chamomile blossoms—*for light brown or blond hair.*
Sage or rosemary—*for dark hair.*
Lavender or basil—*for any hair type.*

INGREDIENTS:

8 cups water
1 cup fresh herbs (1/2 cup if dried)

1. Bring the water almost to a boil. Remove from heat and stir in herbs. Cover and let steep for 2 hours.

2. Strain mixture.
3. To use, simply pour the herbal rinse over your hair as the final step after shampooing. Do not rinse out.
4. Store any leftover rinse in the refrigerator and use within 1 week.

YIELD: 1 QUART

Chapter 8

 geolego

Herbal Flower Arranging

> *The joy of being able to cut flowers freely, lavishly, to decorate the house and to give to friends is an end that justifies a lot of gardening effort.*
>
> —T. H. Everett

Flower arranging is a fun way to express creativity and bring a bit of the garden indoors for others to enjoy. By adding freshly cut herbs to floral arrangements, you can create unusual designs which make memorable impressions on family and friends. Herbs are terrific as floral bouquets because they hold up well and they add their own unique texture, fragrance, and charm.

There is no reason to feel intimidated about flower arranging. You can easily create charming arrangements on your own with just some basic knowledge and a little practice. The more you practice, the better you will get. You don't have to be a professional floral designer in order to create impressive arrangements. However, if you feel you need extra help, enroll in a floral design class at your local community college or park/recreation center. You will soon discover that flower arranging is an extremely re-

warding craft because it is a celebration of the garden and gives
pleasure to everyone who sees your work.

SUGGESTED MATERIALS AND TOOLS

Plant Material: Almost all herbs work well in flower arrangements. Add cut flowers and other greenery to your herbs for
added interest and color.

Floral Foam: This material is sometimes referred to by the brand
name "Oasis." This is a green, spongy material which is used to
hold the cut flowers and provide water. It usually comes in foam
"bricks," which can be purchased at craft stores and floral supply
stores. It can easily be cut with a knife to the desired size. Floral
foam should be soaked for one hour in fresh water before being
used in arrangements.

Scissors/Floral Knife/Clippers: A pair of sharp, clean scissors
or a floral knife is needed for cutting plant material. Garden clippers may be necessary for woody items.

Containers: Just about any container can be used for flower arranging, as long as it is sturdy enough to hold the arrangement

without tipping over. Try using watering cans, teapots, and flowerpots. Be sure to clean containers thoroughly to help reduce bacteria. If baskets or flowerpots are used, line them with papiermâché liners from floral supply stores or plastic trash bags which are cut to size.

Florist Wire: Florist wire is a metal wire which comes on a paddle or spool. It is available in different gauges (thicknesses) from craft stores and floral supply stores. For flower arranging, a 24 or 26 gauge wire is usually sufficient. The wire is used in wreath and garland making and is used to wrap groups of plant material together securely.

Floral Stem Tape: This paper-based tape comes on a roll in either green, brown, or white. It has a sticky surface which is exposed as it is gently stretched. If you wrap it around a small grouping of stems, it sticks to itself and holds the stems together securely without pins. It can also be used to cover a wired stem, thereby hiding the "mechanics."

Green Floral Tape: This is different from floral stem tape. It is more like green masking tape and is found in craft stores and floral supply stores. It is used to tape floral foam into containers. Usually two pieces are taped in a crisscross fashion across the top of the floral foam and onto the container. The tape holds well, even when wet. It is not an essential tool, but can be very helpful with top-heavy arrangements.

Floral Frogs: Sometimes called pinholders or hairpin holders, these small metal objects are set in the bottom of the floral container and help hold the plant stems in place. Some of them look like mini "beds of nails" and the stems are embedded on the spiked ends. Others are just made of metal meshing that allows the stems to poke through. They come in all shapes, sizes, and colors. You can sometimes find used ones at garage sales for a few cents. You can purchase new ones at floral supply stores. They are usually only a few dollars, depending upon the size.

PREPARING YOUR PLANT MATERIAL

Herbs are very long-lasting in water and floral foam. However, it is important to note that in order for any plant material to hold up well, it must be picked and conditioned properly before being arranged.

Pick your materials in the morning, after the morning dew has dried but before the heat of the day hits them. Cut the stems at a 45-degree angle to obtain a maximum surface for water absorption. Use very sharp scissors or a sharp florist knife to cut stems. For woody stems such as rosemary, use pruning shears. Remove the foliage on the bottom half of the stems. After cutting, immediately place the plants in a bucket of room temperature water (not ice cold).

CONDITIONING

Conditioning means to process the plant material so that it will last longer in the arrangement. Usually this means soaking the plant material in water for several hours to rehydrate and prevent shock. But for really long-lasting arrangements, a chemical floral preservative may be added to the water to feed the plants and prevent bacteria from forming. Using a commercial chemical preservative is an optional step. (*Do not use a chemical preservative on any herb or flower to be eaten!* Use it only on plant material to be arranged.)

Commercial preservatives can be purchased from floral supply stores, nurseries, or even your local florist. Each brand comes with instructions on how much preservative to add to your water. Let your herbs and flowers soak in this preservative solution for several hours or overnight and use the mixture to water your finished arrangement.

> ## WHAT IS IN A COMMERCIAL FLORAL PRESERVATIVE?
>
> 1. Antibacterial agents (bacteria will clog pores of the stems and cause arrangements to wilt faster).
> 2. Dextrose (to feed the plants).
> 3. Acidifiers (acidity inhibits bacteria growth).
>
> You can make your own floral preservative by adding 1 teaspoon household bleach to each gallon of water! Although this will not feed the plants, it will keep the bacteria levels down.

CARE OF FLORAL ARRANGEMENTS

1. Keep fresh flowers out of direct sunlight.
2. Change the water frequently to prevent bacteria buildup.
3. Recut the stems in vase arrangements once per week.

BASIC FLORAL DESIGN STEPS

1. Prepare your container for the arrangement; i.e., clean it and add floral foam.
2. Place in your greenery and/or your tallest plant material to give an outline of the arrangement. This will determine the size and shape of your finished design. Work within this outline.
3. Begin adding flowers and herbs to fill in the outline. Don't crowd your flowers. (This is a tough one, because the tendency is to put *all* the flowers you have in one arrangement.) Of course, you don't want to waste the beautiful plant material, but try to use restraint. Place the leftover flowers in a small vase.
4. Pay attention to the textures of the plant material. By varying the textures you get a more interesting design.

5. Use odd (rather than even) numbers of flowers. They are easier to work with and they form a more pleasing pattern.
6. Place larger, heavier flowers at the heart or center of your
   design.
7. Place smaller, brighter flowers at the outer edges.

Design Shapes

Flower arrangements can be made in many different shapes,
but there are four designs which lend themselves to herbal arranging: round, triangular, S-curved, and vegetative.

1. *The Round or Oval Arrangement:* This is the type of
arrangement you see used as a centerpiece or coffee table dis-
play because it looks good from all angles. The trick to making
a nice round arrangement is to make all the stems appear as
though they are radiating from one central point.

© Copyright Theresa Loe

2. *The Triangular and L-shaped Arrangement:* Triangular arrangements are great against walls and in corners. When
you step back and look at this arrangement, it has a very clear
triangle outline. It should be equally balanced on both sides and
the stems should appear to radiate from one central point. An
L-shaped arrangement is basically 1/2 of a triangular arrangement. It is asymmetrical with the heavy, dark-colored flowers
placed toward the center.

© Copyright Theresa Loe

3. ***The S-Shaped Arrangement:*** **Sometimes called a** *Hogarth Curve,* **this type of design resembles a very curvy** *S.* **It must be designed on a pedestal or stemmed container like a candlestick. The heavy, darker flowers should be at the center with wispy greenery forming the** *S.*

© Copyright Theresa Loe

4. *The Vegetative Arrangement:* This casual design style is also known as a *garden grouping* or *cottage garden* design. The arrangement resembles a miniature garden and appears to be growing out of the container. They are best displayed against a wall. Short greenery and leaves are placed around the edges of the container to conceal the floral foam. Then each variety of flower or herb is placed in small groupings as if they are growing in clusters. Tall, vertical groupings are placed toward the back, first. Shorter groupings are then placed toward the front. The plants intermingle to form a "cottage garden" look. Avoid exotic flowers. Use cottage plants in soft pastel colors such as feverfew, delphinium, oregano, roses, and carnations.

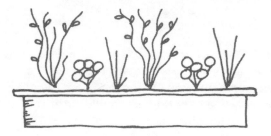

© Copyright Theresa Loe

BASIC ROUND ARRANGEMENT FOR BEGINNERS

This arrangement is very simple to make and looks quite lovely on a coffee table or as a centerpiece. The container should be a very pretty bowl with high sides, such as a crystal candy bowl, round flower vase, or rose bowl. You will need five medium- to large-sized flowers such as lilies, carnations, roses, and gardenias. They will be the main focus of the arrangement. Your greenery (or background material) will be herbal. Sage, marjoram, artemisia, or oregano are perfect choices for the greenery. Variegated varieties such as golden sage are even better! The accent material will also be herbal (accent material is anything that is light and airy such as baby's breath). Try using the seed heads of fennel, dill, salad burnet, or parsley as your accent material.

This arrangement calls for a floral frog (*see* "Suggested Materials and Tools" above). If you do not have one, you can still make the arrangement. A frog just makes it a little easier to keep the greenery in place. But it is not necessary.

MATERIALS:

1 crystal or glass bowl
5 flowers (see above)
greenery material (see above)
few sprigs of accent material (see above)
1 small flower-arranging frog
clippers

1. Cut and condition all of your plant material. Make sure that your container and floral frog are clean.
2. Cut your greenery to about 4–6 inches long and place it in your container. Continue until the entire container is loosely filled (not packed) with the greenery material. (Be sure to keep the arrangement in a round shape.)
3. Cut each flower to about 4–6 inches long. Place it in the container so that each flower is evenly space throughout the greenery.
4. Add a few sprigs of your accent material and you are done!

FRESH HERBAL WREATHS

Decorating with wreaths has origins in ancient cultures all over the world. Wreaths symbolized everything from "good luck" to "victory." Today, they are usually hung on front doors or walls as a symbol of hospitality and welcome. If they are laid flat on a table, wreaths can become centerpieces and punch bowl decorations. By using fresh herbs and flowers from the garden, you can create inexpensive, colorful, and aromatic versions of this old-time decoration. The other advantage to using fresh herbs is that they can be allowed to dry right on the wreath base, which then creates a fragrant, long-lasting dried flower decoration. By adding a few dried flowers or a ribbon, you have a decoration that will last a year or more.

© Copyright Wheeler Arts

A wreath is not just a Christmas decoration. It can be made anytime of the year and is actually most delightful in the spring and summer. It is during this time that the garden is at its peak and the choices of plant material are endless. Easter wreaths, May Day wreaths, and Mother's Day wreaths are fun to create and they add a new twist to each holiday.

Plant Material: Most herbs do very well in wreaths, with the exception of some delicate herbs such as basil, borage blossoms, dill, and fennel. If you use these delicate herbs, their foliage will wilt quickly. More durable herbs would be bay, borage leaves, feverfew, hyssop, lamb's ears, lemon verbena, marjoram, mint, oregano, rosemary, sage, santolina, savory, southernwood, sweet woodruff, tarragon, thyme, wormwood, and yarrow. Any type of woody plant usually does well also. Feverfew is excellent in all types of flower-arranging projects. The flowers hold up very well both in and out of the water.

Wreath Base: The wreath base is the framework of the wreath. It can be a heavy wire circle, a floral foam wreath, a grapevine wreath, a moss or straw wreath, etc. You can purchase the wreath base at a floral supply or craft store. (Mail-order sources are given in the "Source Guide.") You can also fashion your own out of heavy twigs and wire. Many people prefer the grapevine or straw wreath bases because they are sturdy and natural looking.

MATERIALS:

several small buckets of fresh plant material
one 10–12-inch wreath base
1 paddle or spool of 24 gauge florist wire
garden clippers
ribbon

1. Pick your plant material and place it in small buckets of water until you are ready to design your wreath. Cut the plant material so that each sprig is about 6 inches long. For an interesting design, you may want to choose several different textures and shades of green herbs. If herbs such as feverfew, hyssop, mint, marjoram, and thyme are flowering, be sure to include them for extra color.
2. Wrap a length of wire around your wreath base and twist it securely. Do not cut the wire. You are going to use this wire to wrap each bundle of herbs onto the base in one continuous piece.
3. Take a handful of one herb variety (about 5–8 stems, depending upon its size) and lay it on the wreath base. Wrap the spool of wire around the bundle's stems once or twice to secure it. Pull tightly.
4. Take another small handful of a different herb and lay it in the same direction on the wreath base so that its leaves cover the stems of the first bundle. Wrap the wire around to secure it. Sometimes you will need to lay bundles next to each other in order to cover the sides of the wreath base. Continue in this manner until you have covered the entire base with herbs. To attach the last bundle, lift the leaves of the first bundle and tuck the stems underneath. Wrap as usual.

5. Tie off the wire by wrapping it several times and twisting it around itself to secure. Make a loop of wire and attach it to the back so that the wreath can be hung easily.

The technique described here can be used to create a dried wreath too! Instead of attaching fresh bundles of herbs, use dried bundles of herbs. Incorporate a few pods, dried flowers, and ribbon to give a festive look.

GARLAND

Oh Brignal banks are wild and fair,
And Greta woods are green,
And you may gather garlands there
Would grace a summer queen.

—Sir Walter Scott, 1813

Garlands have been used as decorations since ancient times but they became popular in America during the Colonial era. Frugal housewives made garlands of fruits and vegetables and hung them to dry—this was one way to preserve food for the harsh winters. Later, garlands became popular Christmas decorations as well. Today, garlands can be used to decorate windows, fireplaces, mirrors, tables, and even hats all year round! They are popular at weddings and garden parties too.

There are several different ways to make a garland. One of the easiest is to attach bundles of fresh herbs to a rope or string. A long rope can be used to make a swag and a short string can be wrapped around a hat base. Use the same plant material that is described in "Fresh Herbal Wreaths," above. For this technique of garland making, you need foliage that can hold up fairly well out of water.

MATERIALS:

1/4-inch-thick rope or cording cut to desired length
fresh herb sprigs cut 3–5 inches long
other decorations such as straw flowers, fresh flowers,
  baby's breath, etc.
Spool or paddle of florist wire, 24 or 26 gauge
ribbon for the ends

1. Tie a knot onto each end of the rope and then tie one end of the rope to a stationary object, such as a doorknob or post.
2. Beginning at the end that is tied to the stationary object, gather a small bundle of cut herbs and lay them on the rope with the cut ends pointing toward to you. Wrap the wire around the ends of the herbs several times to secure them onto the rope. Do not cut the wire; just leave it on the spool as you work. Take another small handful of herbs and lay them in the same direction so that their leaves cover the wired stems of the first bundle. Wrap the wire around their stems several times to secure them to the rope. Continue in this fashion, working down from the tied end of the garland. As you work, you can add baby's breath, straw flowers, or fresh cut flowers throughout the garland.
3. When you reach the end of the garland, tie off the wire. Add a large, festive bow to each end of the rope. Once hung, the garland will look fresh for about three days to one week (or longer), depending upon the plant material used and the climate. (Obviously, high temperatures will dry out the garland faster.)

TOPIARY

Creating a topiary or standard from a live plant has been a popular gardening technique for hundreds of years. It involves meticulous pruning and care. However, you can create a freshly cut topiary in just a few minutes with plant material from the garden.

The results may last for only a week or two, but you don't have to put in months of pruning to achieve it.

A topiary like this one can be used as a centerpiece or hallway decoration. If you make a fragrant pair of topiaries, you can set them on either side of a doorway or mirror. Craft cement, called plaster of Paris, is used in this project because it cures quickly. It is available at craft supply stores. It not only holds the doweling "stem" in place, but adds weight to the bottom of the pot, which prevents toppling over. Once you make the topiary structure, it can be used again and again throughout the year. Just add fresh floral foam and plant material when you need it for a special occasion.

If you can't find plaster of Paris, you can use dry floral foam or sierra foam (for dried flower arranging) in the bottom of the pot to hold the doweling. The only problem with this is that it will not be as sturdy and will not have the added weight to keep it from toppling over. But in a pinch, it will work.

MATERIALS:

2 plastic flowerpot saucers, 4-inch diameter
1 nail
a hammer
one 2–3-foot piece of 1-inch doweling
6–8-inch clay flowerpot
plaster of Paris
1 block floral foam
floral tape to hold down floral foam
hot glue gun
gray Spanish moss
raffia and/or ribbon
several small buckets of plant material, cut into 6–8-inch
   lengths

1. Nail one of the plastic saucers onto one end of the doweling. Set the second saucer inside the first as a liner. This will form the top of the topiary and hold the floral foam without leaking.

2. Place some plastic or paper in the bottom of the clay flowerpot to plug up the hole. Add water to the plaster of Paris (according to the instructions on the bag) and pour it into the flowerpot, leaving 1 inch of space from the top of the pot. Immediately place the doweling into the cement to form the stem of the topiary. Set it aside to dry completely.

3. Cut a piece of the floral foam to fit inside the 4-inch plastic saucer. Soak it in water for at least an hour and then set it in the plastic saucer. Place two pieces of floral tape across the top and onto the saucer in a criss-cross fashion to hold the foam securely.

4. Use the hot glue gun to cover the doweling and bottom of the plastic saucer with moss. You want the doweling to look like a mossy stem and you don't want any of the plastic to show. Place some moss over the cement in the flowerpot to conceal it. (A piece of raffia or ribbon can be glued to the bottom of the saucer and wrapped down the stem to the top of the flowerpot for added interest if you wish.)

5. Begin placing plant material into the floral foam, forming a round ball shape. Be sure to place some greenery over the edge of the saucer to hide the mechanics of the arrangement.

6. Add flowering herbs, flowers, and pods to the arrangement until the topiary is completely filled in. Add a bow if you wish.

7. Water the topiary lightly every day and keep it out of direct light. It should last for a week or more (just like a regular flower arrangement).

Chapter 9

❧❧❧

Scenting the Home

There are many old-fashioned ways to bring fragrance into the home with herbs. One of the oldest is through the use of potpourri. Potpourri is an aromatic mixture of flowers, herbs, spices, and essential oils which can be used to scent and freshen a musty room, closet, or drawer. Although the term *potpourri* was not specifically used for this preparation until the about eighteenth century, the practice of making aromatic mixtures, like potpourri, dates back to ancient Egypt. Since the Victorian Era, potpourri recipes have become an increasingly popular way to add fragrance to the home. However, there are many other ways to scent the home, and the recipes in this chapter go beyond typical potpourri recipes. They offer new ways to use potpourri, freshly cut herbs, and fragrant essential oils.

Using herbs to scent the home is not only a great way to bring in the outdoors, it's practical too! It's nice to use these aromatic recipes rather than relying on commercial products which use synthetic fragrances and chemicals. The all-natural preparations are far superior in scent, and they are inexpensive to make. For example, some herbs such as lavender and pennyroyal have insect-repelling qualities and can be used by themselves or in potpourri mixtures to repel certain bugs. They can be hung fresh in cupboards, sprinkled over a pet's bedding, or tucked in with woolen articles. Their fragrance will beat out commercially made moth balls any day of the week!

TERMINOLOGY

Fixatives: In perfumery and potpourri making there is one important ingredient which helps the product retain its scent for longer periods of time. This ingredient is called a *fixative.* It is especially important to use a fixative when you are making potpourri as sachets or moth repellants because they must last for longer than a few weeks. The fixative will "fix" or "hold" the scent of the mixture.

There are several natural materials which have fixative characteristics. For many years, the most common fixative was orris root *(Iris germanica),* which is the tuber of the Florentine iris. It is an excellent fixative and is readily available from craft and fragrance supply companies. However, many people are allergic to orris root (especially in powdered form). It can cause red, irritated eyes and an itchy nose. If you are not allergic to orris root, you will find that it is a superior product. But if you are making fragrant products to sell or give as gifts, you may want to use an alternate fixative.

There are several other plants, resins, and barks which can be used as fixatives in recipes, such as oakmoss *(Evernia prunastri)*, cellulose fiber (corn cobs), calamus root/sweet flag *(Acorus calamus)*, gum benzoin *(Styrax benzoin)*, patchouli *(Pogostemon cablin)*, and cedar chips. You can substitute one of the above-mentioned fixatives for orris root in any recipe. For quick, primitive recipes, such as vacuum cleaner sachets, you can even use vermiculite (from your local garden center) as an inexpensive fixative. But vermiculite is limited in its fixative qualities and is not appropriate for potpourris which are to be seen. (It looks tacky and strange.)

Oakmoss has a woodsy scent and is one of the most popular alternatives to orris root. As with all the fixatives listed in this chapter, it can be purchased through mail-order. Cellulose fiber is a fairly new fixative on the market and is made from cut or ground corn cobs. It is very absorbent and you may need to increase the amount of essential oil you use in order to get a strong fragrance. You will find most of the abovementioned fixatives in two forms: cut/sifted or powdered. The cut form is usually best because the powdered form tends to leak from sachets and create a dusty film. The cut form also seems to hold the fragrance longer.

You will notice that some of the potpourri recipes in this chapter include a fixative. Others are either not potpourri or are for immediate use (such as "simmering herbs") and therefore do not need a fixative.

Sachets: Sachets are small bags or bundles filled with potpourri, perfumed powder, or just fragrant herbs. The Victorians called them "sweet bags." There are several things you can use to package sachets. For a simple sachet, you can place several spoonfuls of the mixture in the middle of a cheesecloth square or a fabric square, which is then tied with string. Or you can purchase cotton tea bags to fill with your herb mixture (*see* the "Source Guide" for mail-order sources). For a more romantic look, you can place some of the sachet mixture inside an antique handkerchief and tie it closed with a festive ribbon. If you have the time to sew, rectangular fabric bags are quite charming when filled with potpourri and tied with ribbon. No matter how the sachet is packaged, it will smell wonderful and add a bit of the garden to your home.

Sweet Bags

These sweet bags are just general, all-purpose sachets, filled with the sweet fragrances of the garden. They can be used to perfume drawers, closets, and cupboards that are filled with linens, clothes, or stationery. Sweet bags can also be hung on bedposts, doorknobs, or the backs of chairs to add fragrance to the room.

A sweet bag is definitely worth making for yourself or a dear friend. It also makes an excellent present for someone who is ill or bedridden. When tucked inside bed pillows, it cheers them up with the wonderful perfumes of the outdoors. Since a sweet bag is more likely to be seen, you should make it out of old hankies or pretty pieces of fabric. Keep your eye out for such items at flea markets and garage sales.

Recipe 1: Lemon Sweet Bag

MATERIALS:

1/2 cup oakmoss, cut and sifted
8 drops essential oil of lemon
4 drops essential oil of lavender
1 cup dried lemon verbena leaves
1/2 cup dried lemon grass leaves
1/2 cup dried rosemary leaves
4 handkerchiefs or 6 eight-inch squares of fabric
matching ribbon

Recipe 2: Sweet Woodruff Bag

MATERIALS:

1/2 cup oakmoss, cut and sifted
6 drops rose oil or rose geranium oil
4 drops carnation or cinnamon oil
1 1/2 cups dried sweet woodruff
1 cup dried rose-scented geranium leaves
1 vanilla bean, chopped into pieces
1 tbsp. whole allspice
1 tbsp. whole cloves
5 handkerchiefs or 6–8 eight-inch squares of fabric
matching ribbon

1. Choose one of the recipes above and gather the ingredients. In a medium-sized glass jar with a tight-fitting lid, combine oakmoss with the essential oils. Shake well. Set aside for 3 days to infuse the oakmoss with essential oil fragrance.
2. Add the remaining ingredients to the jar and shake well. Set aside for at least 2 weeks to allow the fragrances to blend. Fill the handkerchiefs or fabric squares with a few heaping spoonfuls of the sachet mixture. Tie securely with ribbon.

YIELD: 4–8 SWEET BAGS

Moth-Repelling Sachets

Long before we had insecticides and moth balls, herbs were used to help deter insects from the household. Recipes using insect-repelling herbs were passed down from mother to daughter for centuries. Moth-repelling herbs were probably considered the most valuable because many families had articles of woolen clothing that they could not afford to lose to hungry moths.

Today, moths can still be a problem and there are many aromatic materials which can be combined to successfully keep these little critters at bay. I like to make these sachets in the spring when I am packing up my sweaters for the summer. Moth-repelling materials include cedar chips, eucalyptus leaves, lavender, patchouli leaves, pennyroyal, santolina, and southernwood. Small, inexpensive bags of cedar chips can be purchased at a pet store, where they are sold as pet bedding. Patchouli leaves have an earthy scent and have fixative qualities as well as moth repelling characteristics. Santolina has a very strong fragrance and should be used in moderation or it can be overpowering in a moth sachet. All the plants mentioned can be collected and dried at home or purchased through mail-order. (Cotton tea bags are also available through mail-order.)

Recipe 1: Lavender Moth Repellant

*1/2 cup cut oakmoss, cut orris root, or crushed patchouli
  leaves
15 drops essential oil of eucalyptus or lavender
1 cup dried lavender blossoms
1 cup dried eucalyptus or pennyroyal leaves
1 cup cedar shavings
10–12 cotton tea bags or 10–12 eight-inch squares of fabric
string (if using fabric)*

Recipe 2: Woodsy Moth Chaser

1/2 cup cut oakmoss, cut orris root, or crushed patchouli
*   leaves*
15 drops essential oil of cedar, pine, or eucalyptus
1 cup dried southernwood
1/2 cup dried santolina
1 cup cedar shavings
1 tbsp. whole cloves
2 whole cinnamon sticks, crushed
8–10 cotton tea bags or 8–10 eight-inch squares of fabric
string (if using fabric)

1. Choose one of the recipes above and gather the ingredients. In a large glass jar with a tight-fitting lid, combine oakmoss, orris root, or patchouli with the essential oil. Shake well and set aside for 1 week.
2. Add the remaining ingredients to the jar. Stir well. Set the mixture aside for another 2 weeks so that the fragrances can blend.
3. After 2 weeks, stuff the tea bags or fabric squares with the moth-repelling mixture and tie closed. For maximum protection, place at least 2 bags in each of your drawers. Use 3–4 bags in closets. Occasionally squeeze the bags to release the fragrance. Replace the sachets each year with fresh ones. The old moth sachets can be replenished with a fragrant essential oil and used as general drawer sachets.

YIELD: **8–12** SACHETS

Carpet Freshener
❦

There are many commercial carpet fresheners on the market which are sprinkled over the carpeting and vacuumed up. The problem with these fresheners is that their scent is very artificial and overpowering. They are also expensive to use all the time. One solution is to create a homemade freshener using baking soda and pure essential oils. This recipe uses lavender or rosemary, but you can substitute your favorite essential oil, if you wish. If you have pets, add a few drops of pennyroyal oil to help deter fleas.

MATERIALS:

4 cups baking soda
2 tsp. ground cloves
20 drops pure essential oil of lavender or rosemary

1. Combine all ingredients in a glass jar with a tight-fitting lid. Shake well. Let mixture set for 24 hours before using.
2. To use: Pour a small amount of the freshener into a fine sieve. Gently shake the sieve over your carpeting, dispersing a light layer of the freshener. Wait 10–15 minutes and then vacuum as usual. Keep any unused freshener in an airtight container.

YIELD: 4 CUPS

FLEA POWDER FOR PET'S BEDDING

Pennyroyal is known for its flea-repelling qualities. Combine 1 cup of baking soda with 10 drops of pennyroyal oil. Follow the instructions above for sprinkling the powder over the pet's bedding areas. Vacuum or shake out their bedding area after about 15–20 minutes. Pennyroyal oil can be very irritating to the skin if not diluted. Do *not* use the pure oil directly on your pet!

Vacuum Bag Sachet

༄ᵒᵉᵒ°ᵣ

As you vacuum, the bag fills with animal hair and debris and can give off an unpleasant odor. One way to eliminate this problem (and freshen the air as you vacuum) is to place a vacuum sachet inside the vacuum bag. Keep a small jar of sachets next to your vacuum bags and toss one inside every time you replace the bag. Use a combination of several dried, aromatic herbs such as lavender, lemon balm, lemon grass, lemon verbena, mint, rose, rosemary, scented geranium, or sweet woodruff.

This recipe calls for vermiculite, which is an ingredient in soil mixtures for potted plants. It is a mica-type mineral which was heated until it expanded into accordion-shaped particles. These particles are very absorbent. In soil, they help retain water. But when used in this unconventional way, they help retain the scent of the sachet. You can purchase small bags of vermiculite at your local garden center.

MATERIALS:

1 cup vermiculite
1 cup baking soda
15 drops of essential oil of mint, lavender, or
    eucalyptus
1 cup dried herbs, crushed (see list above)
3 cinnamon sticks, crushed
10–12 cotton tea bags or 10–12 eight-inch squares of
    heavy cheesecloth
thin string or twine (if using cheesecloth)

1. Combine vermiculite, baking soda, and essential oil in a glass jar with a tight-fitting lid. Cover and shake well. Set aside for 3 days.
2. In a large bowl, combine the ingredients in the jar with the dried herbs and cinnamon. Stir well. If using tea bags, fill

them with the mixture and tie the drawstring closed. If using cheesecloth, place a few spoonfuls of the herb mixture in the center of each cheesecloth square. Draw up the sides and tie with a piece of string.

3. Place one sachet inside the vacuum bag each time you replace it. Store all unused sachets in an airtight container.

YIELD: **10–12** SACHETS

Simmering Herbs

One of the easiest and quickest ways to scent the home is with simmering herbs. By boiling water which is infused with herbs and spices, you release the fragrance quickly into the air with the steam. In just a few minutes, the entire house will smell wonderful. This is a nice way to freshen your home before a party. Just be sure to set a timer so that you do not forget about the herbs and allow the pan to boil dry!

The measurements given here are approximations. You can add or subtract different herbs and spices to get various fragrances. Try using basil, lavender, lemon balm, lemon grass, lemon verbena, mint, rose, rosemary, scented geranium, or sweet woodruff to create your own recipes.

Recipe 1: Lemon

> *3 cups water*
> *1 cup mixed fresh herb leaves of lemon verbena, lemon balm, and lemon-scented geranium*
> *1 strip of fresh lemon or orange peel*
> *2 sticks of cinnamon (or 1 tsp. ground)*
> *1 tsp. whole cloves (or 1/2 tsp. ground)*
> *10 drops of lemon or orange essential oil*

Recipe 2: Vanilla Rose

3 cups water
1 cup fresh rose petals
1/2 cup fresh rose geranium leaves
1/2 vanilla bean, chopped
1 tsp. whole allspice (or 1/2 tsp. ground)
1/4 tsp. vanilla extract

Recipe 3: Lavender

3 cups water
1/2 cup dried lavender blossoms
10 drops lavender essential oil

Recipe 4: Holiday

3 cups water
1 cup fresh rosemary leaves
1/2 cup mixed pine needles
1/2 cup fresh-cut juniper pieces (tips of branches)
2 whole cinnamon sticks, crushed (or 1 tsp. ground)
1 tsp. whole cloves (or 1/2 tsp. ground)
5 drops rosemary or pine essential oil

1. Combine all the ingredients from one of the recipes above in a small sauce pan and bring to a boil.
2. Reduce the heat and let the mixture simmer for 15–20 minutes. Set a timer so that you don't forget to turn it off! You can reuse the mixture several times, but you may have to add more water.

And still she slept an azure-lidded sleep,
In blanched linen, smooth, and lavender'd.

—John Keats

Clothes Dryer Sachet

Nice alternatives to commercial dryer sheets, with their artificial fragrance, are clothes dryer sachets. Although they will not prevent static like the store-bought brands, they do make the clothes sweet-smelling. They can be made out of fabric squares or old cotton socks. (Children's socks are best because they are the perfect size for about 1/4 cup of the sachet mixture.) Cotton tea bags can also be filled with the sachet mixture. One dryer sachet will last for several loads. The heat from the dryer will release the fragrance of the herbs, giving your clothes a springtime scent.

If you choose to make fabric sachets, be sure to use white fabric. Colors might bleed on the wet clothes.

MATERIALS:

1 cup dried lavender blossoms
1/2 cup dried rosemary blossoms
1/2 cup dried lemon verbena
10 drops lavender essential oil
8 eight-inch squares of white cotton fabric or 8 small
  cotton socks
cotton string or white ribbon

1. Combine the dried herbs and the essential oil in a medium-sized bowl. Mix well.
2. If using fabric squares, place approximately 1/4 cup of the herb mixture in the center of each fabric square. Pull up the sides of the square and tie closed with the string or ribbon. If using socks, fill each sock with 1/4 cup of the mixture and tie closed with string or ribbon.
3. Store the sachets in an airtight container. Use one sachet at a time in the clothes dryer with each load. The sachet may be used many times before it loses its scent. Be sure to crush it

in your hand a few times before each use to release the aromatic oils of the herbs.

YIELD: APPROXIMATELY 8 SACHETS

SCENTED DRAWER LINERS

Can't afford those expensive scented drawer liners that are so popular now? Make your own! Choose a cute, inexpensive roll of wallpaper or pick up some old samples from a wallpaper store (they throw out old designs periodically). Open the wallpaper, facedown, onto a long table and sprinkle some dried herbs all over it. (Try dried lavender, lemon verbena, mint, or rosemary.) Then, place 5–6 cotton balls which have been dipped in your favorite essential oil on the paper. (Lavender oil is excellent for this project.) Roll the wallpaper up (with the herbs and cotton balls enclosed) and place it inside a plastic trash bag. Seal the bag shut. Set it aside for 2–3 weeks. Then, unroll the paper and discard the herbs and cotton balls. Cut the paper to fit inside your clothing drawers or linen closet. (You may need to use tacks in the corners to get the paper to lie flat.)

Closet Bouquets

Closet bouquets are nice to use when you are having house guests. They are small bouquets of mixed, fresh-cut herbs which are tucked inside closets or set on top of linens to freshen them. Place them all around a guest room to give your guest a fragrant and pretty welcome present. These small bouquets can also be tucked into luggage for traveling. The traveler will arrive at his or her destination with a suitcase full of fragrance. Just be sure to wrap the bouquets in a thin towel or tissue paper before packing, to prevent them from soiling clothes.

Use the most aromatic herbs you can and be sure to include a few flowers for color. Try using basil, chamomile blossoms, lavender, lemon balm, lemon verbena, mint, rose, rosemary, sage, scented geranium, thyme, sweet woodruff, and yarrow. For added moth-repelling qualities, include pennyroyal, southernwood, or wormwood.

MATERIALS:

several small bunches of fresh herbs (see list above)
rubber bands
ribbon

1. Assemble several small bouquets of the fresh herbs. (Be sure to use several different kinds of aromatic herbs.) Wrap the ends of the bouquets with rubber bands and tie with a ribbon bow.
2. Set the bouquets in drawers, on closet shelves, and on top of bathroom towels.

CAR BOUQUETS

Try making one of the closet bouquets described above and setting it inside your car to make it sweet smelling! Just set it on the dashboard. In the summer, the heat of the sun will completely dry the bouquet in about 24 hours and give the car a wonderful springtime fragrance. After a week, you can remove the bouquet and use it as a fireplace herb or add it to a potpourri recipe!

Fireplace Herbs

Fireplace herbs are small bundles of dried herbs which are tossed into a burning fire to release their fragrance while they burn. These bundles can be made out of leftover herb twigs after the leaves are removed for other purposes, or they can be 4-6-inch branches which are cut and dried specifically for this purpose. Many of the aromatic herbs make good fireplace bundles. Try using basil, lavender, lemon grass, lemon verbena, mint, rosemary, or sage.

MATERIALS:

4-6-inch dried branches of aromatic herbs
cotton string

Tie the dried herb branches into small bundles using the cotton string. Toss one or two bundles into a fire whenever you want to release a smoky herbal fragrance into the room.

Chapter 10

Herbal Treasures

The pleasure one gets from an herb garden is increased many times over when that garden is somehow shared with others. Herbal treasures are crafts, gifts, and wrapping techniques which allow the colors and textures of the garden to be shared with friends and family. As you grow your own herbs, you will want to use them in every decorative way possible. This chapter explores some of the decorative uses of herbs.

Leaf P*rint* S*tationery*

Herbal stationery is a breeze to make with this technique. Fresh leaves are coated with paint and pressed onto paper, leaving their herbal impression behind. Different shades of green can be blended to create one-of-a-kind note cards and stationery sheets. The best herbs for this project are those with flat leaves and heavy veins such as basil, bay, borage, salad burnet, cilantro, feverfew, lamb's ears, lemon balm, mint, nasturtium, parsley, sage, and scented geranium. All you need to print with these leaves is an all-purpose paint brush. However, if you want to use lacy or unusually shaped foliage (like dill or fennel) in this project, you will probably need to purchase a soft rubber roller called a brayer, to coat the leaves. A brayer is basically a rubber rolling pin with a handle and can be purchased at most craft supply stores.

The first time you try this project, you should practice on scrap paper to get the feel of how much paint you need and how much pressure you should use. Once you have made a few samples, you can move on to the real printing with colored and/or textured paper. Try printing on envelopes too! If you are really brave, you can try using fabric paints to decorate shirts and aprons. This project is so easy that kids can do it too!

MATERIALS:

fresh leaves from one of the herbs mentioned above
newspaper
several paper plates
acrylic or watercolor paints in various greens and grays
a flat, 1/4–1/2-inch-wide paint brush
paper towels
plain stationery and note cards for printing

1. Make sure your leaves are clean, dry, and free from bug bites. Lay the newspapers on your work surface to protect it from

paint. Keep a small stack of newspapers to paint on. If you are using acrylic paint, place several dots of different colored paint (about the size of a dime) onto one of your paper plates. If the paint seems too thick, thin it out with a few drops of water. If you are using watercolors, you can dip the brush directly into the paint and blend the colors on the paper plate.

2. Choose a leaf for your first print. Lay it on a piece of newspaper, facedown, so that the underside (the side with the veins) is facing upward. Use the paint brush to paint a thin layer over the entire underside of the leaf. You can paint part of the stem if you wish or you can leave it unpainted for easy handling.

3. Gently pick up the painted leaf and place it, painted side down, onto a piece of paper. While holding the leaf down with one finger, carefully cover it with a piece of paper towel. Gently press it with your fingers (do not rub). Be careful not to move the leaf or it will smear.

4. Remove the paper towel, and then carefully remove the leaf. You should have a nice impression of the herb. You might be able to make a second impression with the same leaf without repainting.

5. Repeat the printing procedures with various leaves and various colors. Be sure to use a fresh area of the newspaper to paint on. Let the finished stationery dry completely (about 24 hours) before using.

TIPS

- Try blending two or three colors together on one leaf. For a natural look, you can use different shades of green or gray. For an autumn look, you can use various shades of orange and rust.
- For stationery, you can place your prints in several areas: across the top of the page, in the upper left corner and lower right corner, or around the entire perimeter of the page.
- Use heavy paper, folded in half, to make note cards.

- To use a brayer with acrylic paint: Place a small amount of paint on a paper plate. Roll the brayer through the paint several times to get an even coating on its surface. Lay the leaf to be printed, facedown, on a piece of newspaper. Roll the brayer over the leaf several times to coat it. Carefully pick up the leaf and continue with Step 3 above. You can use the brayer on lacy foliage or on flowers such as lavender blossoms.

Planted Herb Basket

A planted basket, filled with fragrant herbs, is a terrific hostess gift or housewarming gift. It can also be a nice alternative to flowers for a sick friend. Long after flowers would have wilted, a planted basket is still lush and green. The leaves can be harvested directly from the basket and used in cooking or brewed for tea.

When choosing the herbs for your basket, keep in mind that the container is shallow. Low-growing herbs that do not have long tap roots are best. Choose very young, immature plants so that they can survive for several months in the confined quarters. Many of the herbs will not be able to reach full maturity in the basket, so be sure to tell the receiver of the gift that the herbs should be transplanted into the garden within 6 months. Pick three or four herbs with various types of foliage for an interesting look. You might want to try basil, chamomile, chives, Corsican mint, feverfew, hyssop, lemon balm, marjoram, mint, oregano, parsley, creeping rosemary, sage, savory, French tarragon, thyme, and sweet woodruff.

MATERIALS:

1 medium to large basket
2 heavy-duty plastic trash bags
potting soil
slow-release fertilizer

several small herb plants (see list above)
ribbon

1. Line the basket with two layers of plastic trash bags. This will make the container watertight. (Don't worry about trimming the plastic to the edge of the basket until after it is filled with soil.)
2. Fill the lined basket with potting soil. Add a small amount of slow-release fertilizer and mix it in well. Carefully trim the plastic to the top of the basket edge.
3. Lightly moisten the soil, being careful not to make it water-logged. (Remember, there are no drainage holes.) Plant your herbs in the basket, placing the tallest herb either in the center or the back of the basket. Tie a large bow and attach it to the basket.
4. The planted basket should be watered only when it is beginning to dry out and should be set in front of a very sunny window where it will get at least 4 hours of sunlight per day.

Dried Herbal Picture Frame

These picture frames are completely covered with natural ingredients from the garden. Gray Spanish moss (available at craft stores or through mail-order) covers the entire frame and acts as a foundation for building small clusters of dried botanicals in the corners. Air-dried or pressed flowers can be added for color. Miniature rose buds which have been allowed to air-dry are especially pretty. Dried bay leaves, chamomile blossoms, lavender blossoms, sage leaves, and thyme are good choices for this project.

You can use an inexpensive frame from a garage sale, thrift store, or discount store. Then, just add a special photo and you have a very inexpensive, yet personal gift for a treasured friend.

MATERIALS:

1 picture frame
Spanish moss
hot glue gun and glue
dried herb leaves and flowers
cinnamon sticks, whole allspice, and star anise

1. Use the hot glue gun to attach the Spanish moss over the entire picture frame. Be sure to cover the outside edges.
2. Glue very small pieces of dried sprigs, leaves, flowers, and spices on the corners of the frame in a pleasing design. Start with the leaves and end with the single flowers and spices.
3. Carefully remove any residual "spider webs" of glue. Keep the frame out of direct sunlight to reduce fading.

PRESSED HERBS

Herb leaves and flowers can be pressed flat until they are completely dry. These pressed plants are little preserved pieces of the garden, which can be used to create very romantic projects and whimsical designs. You don't need an expensive flower press to dry herbs in this way. An old telephone book and a few bricks can do the job just fine. The pressed herbs won't last forever, but they should hold their color for at least a year if they are kept out of direct sunlight.

PRESSING THE PLANT MATERIAL

When you collect your plant material from the garden, choose leaves and flowers that have interesting shapes. Almost all the herbs mentioned in this book work well as pressed leaves and flowers with the exception of rose blossoms, which are too large. (Roses must be separated into individual petals to press.) You may also want to include ferns, pansies, lobelia, and ivy in your plant material.

Lay some of the plant material onto pieces of paper towel. Starting at the back of a telephone book, open a page and lay one of these paper towels inside. Then, carefully fold over some pages and lay down another paper towel of herbs. Continue until all the leaves and flowers are lying on paper towels inside the phone book. Lay two heavy bricks on top of the phone book and set it aside for 1–2 weeks to dry.

Pressed Herb Bookmarks

You can use the herbs and flowers you have pressed to create beautifully laminated bookmarks. They make excellent gifts! All you need is clear plastic, self-sticking paper, which is available at some craft supply stores. You can also use clear plastic shelf paper, which is available at hardware stores. Some craft stores also sell laminating sheets which require the heat of an iron to adhere to paper. These laminating sheets can be easily substituted for the self-sticking paper used in this project.

MATERIALS:

pencil and ruler
heavy white paper
pressed herb leaves and flowers
white craft glue (which dries clear)
paint brush
paper plate
tweezers
clear plastic, self-sticking paper
scissors
hole punch
ribbon

1. Use a pencil and ruler to lightly draw an outline of the bookmark shape you want to create on the paper. Pour some of the white craft glue onto the paper plate and use the paint brush to carefully coat the backside of some of the pressed

herbs with the glue. Position the pressed herbs within the bookmark outline in an attractive design. Gently press the leaves with your fingers. (You may need tweezers for the more delicate herbs.)

2. Continue gluing until your design is complete. Allow the glue to dry for a few hours.
3. Carefully cut out the bookmark along your penciled outline. Cut a piece of clear plastic, self-sticking paper approximately 1/2 inch larger than the bookmark. Carefully peel off the back and place it over the pressed flower bookmark. Smooth out any bubbles. Trim the plastic to match the bookmark edges.
4. Use the hole punch to make a hole in the top of the bookmark. Tie a ribbon through the hole.

Pressed Herbal Candle

Small, pressed herb leaves and flowers are used in this project to decorate a plain pillar candle. Choose a large candle (about 2–4 inches in diameter) so that you have enough surface to work on. Use very flat leaves, sprigs, and flowers such as salad burnet, dill, fennel, ivy, oregano, pansies, parsley, and thyme.

Paraffin wax can be found in the canning section or spice section of many supermarkets. Use extreme caution when melting paraffin wax. It is very flammable.

MATERIALS:

1 box paraffin wax
1 white pillar candle, circular or square
several different pressed leaves and flowers
2 paint brushes, one large and one small

1. In a double boiler, carefully melt the paraffin wax over very low heat. Watch the wax closely! It is very flammable!
2. When the wax is completely melted, remove it from the heat.

Use the wax as "glue" to adhere the pressed leaves and flowers in a decorative design on the sides of the candle. To do this, use the small paint brush to dab wax on the back of each leaf and then press the leaf to the candle. Continue until all the leaves are "glued" to the candle. (You can also use white glue to adhere the leaves to the candle.)

3. Use the larger paint brush to "paint" several layers of wax over the entire surface of the candle. This will seal in your leaves and keep them from falling off. Continue until the entire candle is covered with the paraffin wax.

Pressed Herb Wrapping Paper

For a dramatic effect, wrap a gift in plain white paper or brown postal paper and then decorate it with pressed herbs. (Postal paper is used for mailing packages and gives a country look.) Position your pressed herb designs in the corners of the package. Feverfew blossoms, oregano, rosemary, and sage work especially well on gift wrapping paper. Add a few pressed flowers such as pansies for color. Tie the package with raffia, lace ribbon, or twine so that you do not detract from the herbal design. It takes only a few minutes to spruce up a plain package in this way and the results are very romantic looking.

MATERIALS:

white craft glue (the kind that dries clear)
paper plate
paint brush
a gift wrapped in white or brown paper
pressed herb leaves and flowers
tweezers

1. Pour some of the white craft glue onto the paper plate and use the paint brush to carefully coat the backside of some of the pressed herbs with the glue. Position the pressed herbs

onto the wrapped package and gently press with your
fingers. You may need tweezers for the more delicate herbs.
2. Continue gluing until your design is complete. Allow the glue
to dry for a few hours.

Natural Herbal Gift Wraps

The pressed leaf wrapping paper described above is a great
way to package a gift for a special person. But there are other
ways to wrap and package gifts using herbs and other materials
right out of the garden. Listed below are tips and design ideas for
sprucing up your packages and making gift giving a garden experience.

- Tuck a small fresh or dried herbal bouquet under the bow
  of a wrapped package.
- Tie a fresh or dried herbal sprig onto a bottle of herbal vinegar.
- Dip dried bay leaves in gold paint and wire them onto jars of
  herbal jelly.

DRIED HERB AND SPICE CLUSTERS

After wrapping a package, tie it with something rustic such as
twine, raffia, or paper ribbon. Then use a glue gun to attach air-
dried herb sprigs in a mounding, cluster shape in the center of the
bow. You can use bay, calendula blossoms, feverfew, lamb's ears,
lavender, sage, or thyme. Next, glue on whole nuts (such as wal-
nuts, almonds, and hazelnuts), spices (such as cinnamon sticks and
whole star anise), and various dried pods. If necessary, you can
add a few more herb sprigs to fill in any blank spaces. The result
is a fragrant embellishment that makes the entire gift seem much
more special.

FLORAL VIALS

Floral vials are tiny, pointed containers, with a plastic cap, that hold the stems of fresh plant material. They are used in floral design and act as tiny vases for flowers and leaves. You can purchase them from florists and floral supply stores. You can use these floral vials to make tiny bouquets of herbs which can be tucked into gift baskets or wired onto packages. They will allow the plant material to be used as a decoration for at least 24 hours. They are especially beautiful when used with lace ribbon on wedding presents or bridal shower gifts.

Source Guide

All the companies listed here offer mail-order services. Many of the companies charge nominal fees for their catalog. Since fees are constantly changing, they were not included in this listing. For availability and price information on any of these catalogs, you should send a self-addressed, stamped envelope.

Plants and Seeds

Carroll Gardens
P.O. Box 310
Westminster, MD 21157

The Cook's Garden
P.O. Box 535
Londonderry, VT 05148

The Flowery Branch
P.O. Box 1330
Flowery Branch, GA 30542

Goodwin Creek Gardens
P.O. Box 83
Williams, OR 97544

Heirloom Garden Seeds
P.O. Box 138
Guerneville, CA 95446

Logee's Greenhouse
141 North Street
Danielson, CT 06239

Nichols Garden Nursery
1190 North Pacific Highway
Albany, OR 97321-4580

Rasland Farm
N.C. 82 at U.S. 13
Goodwin, NC 28344-9712

Sandy Mush Herb Nursery
316 Surrett Cove Road
Leicester, NC 28748-9622

Shepherds Garden Seeds
30 Irene Street
Torrington, CT 06790

Territorial Seed Company
P.O. Box 157
Cottage Grove, OR 97424-0061

Well-Sweep Herb Farm
317 Mt. Bethel Road
Port Murray, NJ 07865

Organic Garden Supplies
(Fertilizers, natural pest management, etc.)

Bountiful Gardens
Ecology Action
5798 Ridgewood Road
Willits, CA 95490

Gardens Alive
5100 Schenley Place
Lawrenceburg, IN 47025

The Natural Gardener
8648 Old Bee Caves Road
Austin, TX 78735

**Peaceful Valley Farm
Supply**
P.O. Box 2209
Grass Valley, CA 95945

Worms Way Garden Supply
3151 South Highway 446
Bloomington, IN 47401

Antique Roses

**The Antique Rose
Emporium**
Route 5, Box 143
Brenham, TX 77833

**Roses of Yesterday and
Today**
802 Brown's Valley Road
Watsonville, CA 95076-0398

Vintage Gardens
2227 Gravenstein Highway
South
Sebastopol, CA 95472

Craft Supplies and Botanicals
(Essential oils, bulk botanicals, cosmetic-making supplies, bottles, cotton tea bags, etc.)

Aroma Vera
5901 Rodeo Road
Los Angeles, CA 90016-4312
*(Essential oils and
aromatherapy products)*

**Gabrieana's Herbal
Products**
P.O. Box 215322
Sacramento, CA 95821

*(Essential oils, bulk
botanicals, books, empty
"press 'n' brew" tea bags,
etc.)*

The Glass Pantry
231 Cherry Alley
Maysville, KY 41056
*(Small selection of unusually
shaped glass bottles for
vinegars and cosmetics)*

Lavender Lane
5321 Elkhorn Boulevard
Sacramento, CA 95842
*(Big selection of glass and
plastic bottles, everything you
need for cosmetics, including
essential oils, beeswax pearls,
and heat-sealable tea bags)*

LorAnn Oils
4518 Aurelius Road
P.O. Box 22009
Lansing, MI 48909-2009
*(Essential oils, food crafting,
candle-making supplies)*

Mountain Rose Herbs
P.O. Box 2000
Redway, CA 95560
*(Essential oils, lots of
cosmetic supplies, beeswax,
almond oil, bulk botanicals,
cotton tea bags, books,
bottles)*

Nature's Herb Company
1010 46th Street
Emeryville, CA 94608
*(Essential oils, bulk
botanicals)*

**Jean's Greens Herbal Tea
Works**
RR1, Box 55J, Hale Road
Rensselaerville, NY 12147
*(Tea, essential oils, bulk
botanicals, miscellaneous
herbal products)*

The Scented Garden
P.O. Box 126
Anna, TX 75409-0126
*(Miscellaneous herbal
products, potpourri supplies,
cotton tea bags, salve tins,
teas, botanicals)*

Sunburst Bottle Company
7001 Sunburst Way
Citrus Heights, CA 95621
*(Big selection of glass and
plastic bottles, vials, and jars
which can be used for
vinegar and cosmetics)*

Tom Thumb Workshops
14100 Lankford Hwy. Rt. 13
P.O. Box 357
Mappsville, VA 23407
*(Essential oils, bulk
botanicals, craft and
potpourri supplies,
laminating sheets)*

Herbal Books, Audiotapes and Videotapes

**Country Thyme
Productions**
P.O. Box 3090
El Segundo, CA 90245
*(Videos on home
entertaining, cooking, and
crafting with herbs)*

The Herb Farm
32804 Issaquah-Fall City Road
Fall City, WA 98024
*(Miscellaneous herb products,
books, audiotapes of herbal
instructors)*

Jeanne Rose Aromatherapy
219 Carl Street
San Francisco, CA 94117
*(Herbal books, lecture
information)*

Wood Violet Books
3814 Sunhill Drive
Madison, WI 53704
*(Huge selection of books on
herbal cooking, gardening
and medicinal uses)*

Floral Supplies

**IFAR—Wreath Supply
Company**
2917 Anthony Lane NE
Minneapolis, MN 55418
*(Wreath frames and
supplies)*

**McFadden's Vines &
Wreaths**
Rt. 3, Box 2360
Butler, TN 37640
*(Twig and moss wreath
bases)*

Bibliography

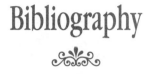

Allardice, Pamela. *Lavender*. London, England: Robert Hale, 1991.

Bremness, Lesley. *Herbs*. New York, New York: Dorling Kindersley, 1994.

Brinton, Diana. *The Complete Guide to Flower Arranging*. London, England: Merehurst Limited, 1990.

Brown, Alice Cooke. *Early American Herb Recipes*. New York, New York: Bonanza Books, 1966.

Cornell Plantations, U. Of California Botanical Garden & Matthaei Botanical Gardens. *Herb Gardening*. New York, New York: Pantheon Books, 1994.

Cox, Janice. *Natural Beauty at Home*. New York, New York: Henry Holt and Company, Inc., 1994.

Cox, Jeff. *Your Organic Garden*. Emmaus, Pennsylvania: Rodale Press, 1994.

Creasy, Rosalind. "Fennel". Loveland, Colorado: *Herb Companion Magazine*, April/May, 1995: 26–31.

DeBaggio, Thomas. *Growing Herbs From Seed, Cutting and Root*. Loveland, Colorado: Interweave Press, Inc., 1994.

Dinsdale, Margaret. *Skin Deep*. Buffalo, New York: Camden House Publishing, 1994.

Drury, Elizabeth. *The Butler's Pantry Book.* New York, New York: St. Martin's Press, 1981.

Facetti, Aldo. *Natural Beauty.* New York, New York: Simon & Schuster Inc., 1991.

Fox, Helen Morgenthau. *Gardening with Herbs for Flavor and Fragrance.* New York, New York: MacMillan Company, 1934.

Foster, Steven. "Aloe Vera". Loveland, Colorado: *Herb Companion Magazine,* Feb/March, 1995: 49-52.

Foster, Steven. *Herbal Renaissance.* Layton, Utah: Gibbs Smith Publisher, 1994.

Freeman, Margaret B. *Herbs for the Mediaeval Household.* New York, New York: The Metropolitan Museum of Art, 1943.

Garland, Sarah. *The Complete Book of Herbs & Spices.* New York, New York: Viking Press, 1979.

Genders, Roy. *Natural Beauty.* London, England: Promotional Reprint Company Ltd, 1992.

Hill, Madalene and Barclay, Gwen. *Southern Herb Growing.* Fredericksburg, TX: Shearer Publishing, 1987.

McDonald, Donald. *Sweet Scented Flowers and Fragrant Leaves.* New York, New York: Charles Scribner's Sons, 1895.

McLeod, Judyth A. *Lavender, Sweet Lavender.* Kenthurst, England: Kangaroo Press, 1992.

McVicar, Jekka. *Jekka's Complete Herb Book.* London, England: Kyle Cathie Limited, 1994.

Michael, Pamela. *All Good Things Around Us.* New York, New York: Holt, Rinehart and Winston, 1980.

Rohde, Eleanour Sinclair. *Herbs and Herb Gardening.* London, England: The Medici Society, Ltd., 1946.

Sanecki, Kay N. *History of the English Herb Garden.* London, England: Ward Lock, 1992.

Sedenko, Jerry. *The Butterfly Garden.* New York, New York: Running Head Books, Inc., 1991.

Siegler, Madeleine H. *Making Potpourri.* Pownal, Vermont: Storey Communications, Inc., 1991.

Simmons, Adelma Grenier. *Herbs Through the Seasons at Caprilands.* Emmaus, PA: Rodale Press, 1987.

Simmons, John V. *The Science of Cosmetics.* London, England: The MacMillan Press, Ltd., 1989.

Stokes, Donald & Lillian. *The Hummingbird Book*. New York, New York: Little Brown and Company, 1989.

Strauch, Betsy. "The Many Faces of Artemisia". Loveland, Colorado: *Herb Companion Magazine*, Oct/Nov. 1993: 24-29.

Tourles, Stephanie. *The Herbal Body Book*. Pownal, Vermont: Storey Communications, Inc., 1994.

Tucker, Arthur O. "Herbs vs. Bugs". Loveland, Colorado: *Herb Companion Magazine*, June/July, 1994: 44-47.

Tucker, Arther O. "Will the Real Oregano Please Stand Up?". Loveland, Colorado: *Herb Companion Magazine*, Feb/March, 1992: 20-27.

Willan, Anne. *La Varenne Pratique*. New York, New York: Crown Publishers, 1989.

Williams, Betsy. *Are There Faeries at the Bottom of Your Garden?* Andover, Massachusetts: Betsy Williams, 1994.

Young, Anne. *Practical Cosmetic Science*. London, England: Mills & Boon Limited, 1972.

Index